Marketing
and **People**

Theme 1 for Edexcel Business AS and A Level

Alan Hewison

Edited by **Brian Ellis**

Alan Hewison is an experienced enthusiast for the courses which have evolved from the Nuffield Economics and Business project. He has taught, examined and written for these courses since their inception.

Brian Ellis has been involved in teaching, examining, curriculum development, teacher training and writing. He sees it as important for people to think and to smile sometimes.

© Anforme Ltd 2015 (Revised 2018)
ISBN 978-1-78014-011-7
Images supplied by Shutterstock.com

Anforme Ltd, Stocksfield Hall, Stocksfield, Northumberland NE43 7TN.

Typeset by George Wishart & Associates, Whitley Bay.
Printed by Stephens & George Print Group, Merthyr Tydfil.

Contents

This book gives a general introduction to the world of business and follows the specification sequence for theme 1 in the Edexcel AS and A Level Business course from 2015. At the end of each of the five specification sections, there is a question in the format to be expected in the Marketing and People exam paper. Four of these are data response questions and there is one section C style extended writing question. Tackling these is intended to be part of the learning process as well as to introduce students to the structure of the exam.

We are very grateful to the businesses which have allowed us to use their experience to give real contexts for business ideas. In the case of small businesses, we have changed names when asked to and have simplified some situations. However, we have tried to stay real rather than rely on fictional case studies.

We are also grateful to everyone, too many people to name, whose ideas have contributed to the earlier books (and courses) on which this is built.

The mistakes herein are ours.

Chapter 1

Meeting customer needs

Online retailing

E-commerce is the fastest growing retail market in Europe. Sales have grown from £132.05bn in 2014 to £262.46bn in 2018.

In Europe in 2018, online retailers are expanding 14.2 times faster than conventional outlets. This creates major problems for store-based retailers.

In the UK, the Centre for Retail Research has predicted that by 2018…

- Total store numbers will fall by 22%, a drop of nearly 62,000.
- Job losses in retailing will be around 316,000 compared to today.
- The share of online retail sales will rise from 12.7% (2012) to 21.5%.

Discussion points

1. Assess the impact these changes might have on…
   (a) consumers; (b) retailers

2. Suggest two strategies a store-based retailer might use to remain competitive

The market

However good a product is, understanding the market is important if a business is to succeed. What happens in a market can determine the price the consumer pays and the revenue that the business earns. It acts as a way of determining what gets produced in an economy and is the signal for businesses to be created or even destroyed.

The market is where buyers and sellers get together and can be defined as…

> A **market** is any medium in which buyers and sellers interact and agree to trade at a price.

Note the use of the word 'medium' as many markets are virtual and although buyers and sellers interact they do not meet face to face. Digital technology has made much of this possible, think of eBay, Amazon or the electronic trading of stocks and shares.

Mass markets and niche markets

Markets come in all shapes and sizes ranging from the very small and local to the huge global markets of the modern world. The size of a market is determined mainly by the number of buyers whose presence causes businesses, which want to make a profit, to enter the market and sell.

> A **niche market** is a small part of the overall market that has certain special characteristics; these may include providing a specialised or luxury product or service. Niche marketing is used when a business focuses on a narrow or small market segment.
>
> A **mass market** is, as its name implies, a very large market with a high sales volume. Mass marketing occurs when one standardised product is aimed at the largest groups of consumers for that particular product or service.

Very large markets are referred to as mass markets and involve a large proportion of the population. A mass market is a term used for the largest groups of consumers for a product or service within the market. It is broad in nature and is not easily categorised by segmentation. The wants of the customers tend to be more general and non-specific, the product or service is often standardised, heavily promoted and available over a wide area.

By contrast niche markets are much smaller, often with a specialised or specific type of product or service. Niche markets only have a small share of the overall market. Customers can be easily segmented, prices tend to be higher and there is often a closer link between buyer and seller. Promotion is likely to be low-key and specifically targeted at the niche customer. Availability is limited by comparison to mass market products.

> Customers are **segmented** when a business divides them into groups, perhaps by income, age or tastes, and tries to cater for their separate preferences.

Markets often contain both mass market producers and niche producers. For example the car market contains mass market manufacturers such as Ford, Toyota and Volkswagen as well as niche manufacturers such as Ferrari, McClaren and Rolls-Royce. Alongside the big supermarkets are numerous specialist food shops, delicatessens and farmers' markets. If you fancy a snack bar you could choose a global brand such as Kit-Kat or a lesser known bar that might be fair-trade or made from organic ingredients.

Figure 1.1: Market niche

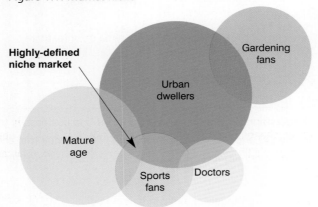

Being a niche producer can be advantageous. There tends to be less outright competition and sometimes none at all. As a result prices are likely to be higher. By being specific in what they produce they are much more likely to be able to satisfy their particular customer's needs, leading to increased loyalty and repeat purchases. Niche producers are often smaller and more flexible and so able to respond quickly to changes in the market.

There is of course a downside, by their very nature there is little room for expansion. Although some niche producers do make the transition to become mass market producers – think about Apple! Producing on a small scale can make niche producers vulnerable to economic downturns and changes in consumer tastes. Successful niche producers can be taken over by bigger businesses.

Mass market producers can benefit from large numbers of customers and high sales revenues. By producing a large output they can benefit from reductions in unit costs. These reductions come from expanding output of a standardised product. For example they may arise from using machinery more efficiently, bulk buying, cheaper finance or better training programmes. Economists call such cost reductions 'economies of scale'.

The downside for the mass market producers is that they often face severe competition and having to be price competitive can lower profit margins. Mass market products and services are usually heavily promoted this means that there are high advertising and promotional costs which reduce profitability.

The rise of the digital economy has also affected these types of market. Niche markets have grown in number as businesses can now have access to a vast number of potential customers that previously would have been unaware of their existence. As a result some mass markets have declined, for example in the music and entertainment sectors.

The holiday market

Thomson, the holiday company, expected nearly one million people to visit their shops or website on 7th January 2017. Some 27,500 customers were then expected to book within 24 hours. Thomson is part of the TUI group, the largest leisure, travel and tourism company in the world. Taking all these holidaymakers away over the coming year, Thomson Airways will carry over 130,000 tonnes of luggage, flying over 107 million miles to 92 holiday destinations.

In the early 1980's, after a period of travelling in Asia, Tim Greening and Glenn Rowley decided to set up a travel company with a difference. Named after their most recent expedition to K2 at the heart of Pakistan's Karakoram Mountains, the company became 'The Karakoram Experience'. Today, as KE Adventure Travel, that same company has grown to become a leading independent adventure travel company specialising in travel to the world's highest peaks, and untamed wilderness areas.

Questions

1. What sort of markets do Thomson and KE Adventure Travel operate in? Explain your answer.
2. Explain the benefits for each company of operating in such a market.
3. Can you see any possible disadvantages?

Dynamic markets

Every business has to adapt to the changing nature of its market. If not, it is likely to get left behind and no longer be competitive. Ultimately, falling sales will cause it to exit the market. Markets change all the time and are said to be dynamic because they are shaped by forces which change frequently.

Some markets are more dynamic than others. Most high-tech products have rapidly changing markets. Here the dynamism has its origins in the changes in technology on the supply side of the market. Some businesses create new products, or new variations of an older product (think of smart phones). Other businesses make well-known products in new ways, with new technologies that help them to cuts costs of production. (Think of salmon – fish farming has cut costs and created a mass market.)

> Markets are said to be **dynamic**. This means that they are constantly changing. Countless decisions made at the individual level by both buyers and sellers alter the nature and behaviour of the market. Sellers respond to the changing needs of buyers by improving existing products and services or introducing new ones. Sellers respond to competitors' changes in order to remain competitive.

Dynamism can start on the demand side of the market too. A change in fashions will lead to rising demand for some products and falling demand for others. Small computer 'netbooks' had three good years before they were overshadowed by 'tablets'. Advertising may change tastes and fashions, or they may change all on their own. Rising incomes can increase demand, especially for luxuries. Demand for some products falls because a more desirable substitute has been found.

Some markets are relatively slow moving, for example the snack confectionery market is dominated by brands. Some are very old – Kit-Kat and Mars bars have survived for 75 years, more or less unchanged, even if new owners take over the business.

> A **stable market** is one in which the pace of change is slow; market size and market share are fairly constant with little variation in price. Innovation is rare and may just consist of minor changes to existing products.

Online retailing

Online retailing is now firmly established in most economies and is rapidly establishing itself in many developing countries. Today, just about anything can be bought online; giant multinational companies such as eBay and Amazon are household names. Businesses of all shapes and sizes offer consumers access to a bewildering variety of goods and services. There is a 'long tail' of niche markets. This development would not have been possible without the growth of technology and the digital economy.

The rise of the digital economy and the impact it has had on businesses and consumers alike cannot be underestimated. By giving access to markets and providing numerous channels that connect buyers and producers all over the globe it has transformed the retail and business world.

> Defining the **digital economy** is not easy; most definitions describe it simply as an 'economy built on digital technologies'. The internet facilitates the use of this technology.

According to Mesenbourg (2001), three main areas of the 'Digital Economy' concept can be identified:

- supporting infrastructure (hardware, software, telecoms, networks, etc.);
- e-business (any process that an organisation conducts over digital networks);
- e-commerce (buying and selling of goods and services).

These three components are inevitably entwined and blurred in today's world and the rise of social media has added another dimension which overlaps with business.

In many areas the digital economy is driving economic growth and creating wealth, it has brought about structural change, altered the face of the traditional high street and given more power to buyers and consumers in their battle with the big producers.

It has not all been positive though, some are beginning to think that the growing power of businesses such as Google and Amazon has become a problem, for example by stifling competition in some markets. When Amazon was instructed that French law made 'free delivery' unacceptable, they quickly introduced a 1 cent delivery charge. They are strong enough to challenge governments.

High Street retailers have not watched idly as their market share has fallen. The problem is least significant for those who sell small perishable items (such as milk and newspapers). Convenience and local availability give them some protection. High Street clothing stores keep an advantage with those who like to try things on and those for whom shopping is a hobby. Potential loss of market share is greatest for durable items, such as electrical and electronic products for example.

Many retailers have built an online presence to combine with their stores. Major supermarkets now deliver orders placed online, saving consumers the chore of shopping. Large retailers now frequently encourage customers to order online, either for delivery or for collection in store. HMV has added HMV Digital to sell downloads and Waterstones sells eBooks (online) as well as hard copy traditional books.

Argos stores are essentially warehouses with front of house ordering areas. Argos now has its catalogue online as well as printed, so customers can 'click and collect'. Another move to exploit online sales is that Argos now advertises some products on eBay. Waiting in for deliveries can be inconvenient, Argos offers other traders the option of delivering to Argos stores so customers can collect from their local store rather than wait in for deliveries. A bonus for Argos is that consumers who 'pop in' to collect items from stores often also make another purchase whilst there.

How markets change

Markets change all the time. They are dynamic, responding to shifts in demand and supply. There are many factors that drive change in the market. The digital economy (see above) is just one factor altering the way markets work, affecting both the producer and the consumer. Change can be driven by the consumer as they seek products and services more specifically suited to their needs; it can be brought about by innovation (see below) or it can be created by government intervention. Markets do not operate in a vacuum; governments create rules and regulations that affect the market and what happens in it. For example the automobile market has been affected by increasing legislation to reduce harmful emissions; exhausts have to be cleaner and car engines less polluting.

Innovation and market growth

Innovation means coming up with new ideas and ways of doing things, producers do this to gain sales or to reduce costs. Being innovative leads to growth for businesses and for some such as Google or Apple it is a key strategy. For pharmaceutical producers (medicines), this is essential as without it they would be left struggling once cheaper rivals copied their products.

> **Product innovation** occurs when new technologies make it possible to create completely new products.

Process innovation can mean not just changes to the way things are produced but other areas such as distribution channels, stock control systems and supply chains.

> **Process innovation** means using new technologies to improve production methods, so that costs are reduced without a loss in quality.

New or improved products can appeal to consumers and increase sales but they can also create whole new markets that rapidly grow. In recent years tablets and smartphones have both become huge global markets. According to the International Data Corporation (IDC), 235.8 million tablets were sold in 2014. This in turn helps the market for 'apps' to grow.

It is not just product innovation that drives market growth. Process innovation can expand markets as well. If costs can be reduced by more efficient methods of production then price may also be reduced, stimulating demand and market growth.

Adapting to change

Businesses cannot afford to stand still; they must take notice of what is happening. Successful businesses must have a range of tactics and strategies to deal with the changes in the market. Their marketing plans can be...

● Offensive, in that they try and increase sales or develop new markets.
● Defensive, in that they react to competition and try to maintain their market share.
● A mixture of both.

> **Marketing** is the action or process of promoting and selling products or services, including market research and advertising. It is how the business connects to its customers.

The objectives of the business will vary. Of course it will want to make a profit. But which is more important, short or long-term gains? If the focus is on the short term, charging a high price may look like a good idea. From a long-term perspective, the business might look to expand, creating a mass market or increasing its market share by keeping prices as low as possible. Becoming more powerful in the market may seem more attractive than making short-term profits. The business may look to improve its products or develop a competitive advantage in some other way. **Marketing** will be an important part of this. It can lead to an increase in market share, whether or not the market is dynamic in other respects. This would be an offensive strategy.

Some of the changes that businesses typically face will be external. A competitor may bring a new product to the market which has many attractive features. To compete, the business will have to rethink its own product strategy. (This will be defensive marketing.) Or costs may rise, threatening all the businesses in this particular market. The winner may be the business that can compete on price, absorbing the cost increases successfully by looking for ways of improving efficiency.

Competition affects all businesses either directly or indirectly.

How competition affects the market

Competition affects all businesses either directly or indirectly. Apple and Samsung are rivals and their smartphones are in direct competition. A suit manufacturer such as Armani is not a direct rival of Apple, but if a consumer buys an iPhone then they may not have enough money to buy a new suit as well. In a general sense, all businesses are competing for our limited disposable income as we have to make choices when spending limited incomes.

Competition in markets is usually thought to be good for the consumer as it makes businesses try harder to make sales. This can mean better products, better service and lower prices. There are beneficial effects for the economy as well.

Figure 1.2: Benefits of competition

In a competitive market businesses must strive against each other to make sales to consumers. This makes them efficient or else they will exit the market.

The consumer benefits from lower prices, greater choice, innovative products, improved reliability and better quality products and service.

The economy benefits as resources are used more efficiently as businesses strive to succeed. Productivity increases and businesses become more competitive internationally, boosting exports and growth.

If competition is predominantly based on marketing, the costs involved in advertising, sponsorship and other forms of promotion can result in higher prices without 'real' gains to consumers. For example, research and development to improve toothpaste benefits consumers, but it is alleged that some top brands spend more on marketing than on research or on the actual contents of their product.

On the other hand, if competition is weak or non-existent this creates problems. Businesses can charge high prices, be relaxed about efficiency and the quality of their products and ignore innovation. This works against the interest of consumers and the economy.

The difference between risk and uncertainty

Risk involves situations where the outcomes are known and can be calculated or quantifiable. When you buy an insurance policy so that you can drive, the insurer has carefully calculated the probability of your having an accident, based on the information available about age, gender, experience and so on. This reduces the risks that the insurance company is taking very considerably. The insurer knows that the outcome of people driving will involve some accidents and they can usually predict how many for any given type and number of drivers. Similarly, accountants can assess the financial risks that a business is taking. Risk can be 'managed' as shown below, and some actions can be rejected as too risky.

Figure 1.3: Risk management

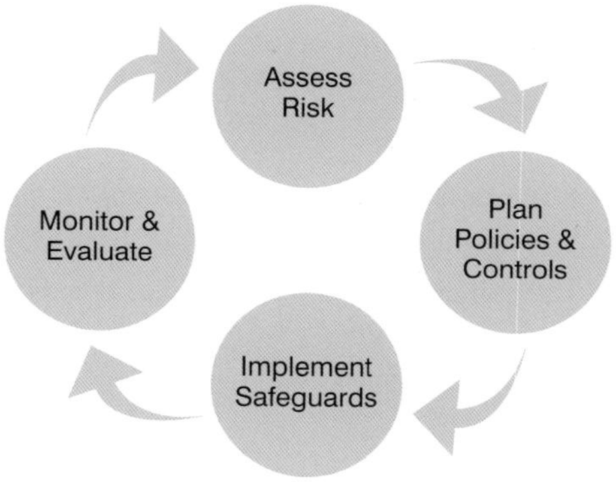

Figure 1.4: Risk and uncertainty

Uncertainty is different because it is caused by factors outside the businesses' control and possible outcomes cannot be calculated with any degree of accuracy. Uncertainty is unpredictable; there are too many unknown variables which make it impossible to estimate what is going to happen. The business may be well aware of these factors but this does not reduce uncertainty. We know that oil prices vary all the time but we cannot calculate what they might be in a year's time. Bad weather can lead to poor harvests and increased food prices but we cannot predict how many bad harvests there might be in the next 10 years. For farmers and consumers this is uncertainty.

> **Risk** is concerned with things that can go wrong where the chance of mishaps can be calculated. Action is possible to reduce risk.
>
> **Uncertainty** is unpredictable and uncontrollable and can create both minor and major problems.

Using information about the kinds of things that might go wrong and how to reduce the damage they can do reduces risk. Wearing hard hats on a construction site and seat belts in cars are obvious examples. Uncertainty produces shocks as well as minor problems. Both are unavoidable and must be dealt with. 'What if' contingency planning can improve a business' reaction, but events from earthquakes and banking collapses to public transport delays cannot be controlled by a business.

> **Contingency planning** is an activity undertaken to ensure that proper and immediate follow-up steps will be taken by a management and employees in an emergency.

Market research

Sian Lang worked as a chef in a pub/restaurant before starting her own catering service. This has expanded to cover weddings, company gatherings and public events. Friends have advised her that her paellas would sell well at The Glastonbury Festival.

This was an attractive opportunity but not an easy one. Over 170,000 people are at Worthy Farm over the long festival weekend. Few of them have the facilities or the inclination to prepare their own food. The potential market is enormous by Sian's standards. However, there are 250 food stalls on site and the conditions laid down are demanding. Her informed estimate was that setting up a decent stall (if her application succeeded), with the festival licence, fitting out and staffing it, would cost her £10,000. Many traders return regularly, suggesting that a profit must still be possible.

Discussion points

How important is it for Sian to undertake market research before applying for a festival licence? How could she gather required information?

The main aim of market research is to provide information about the market that the business can use to make better informed decisions. The information gathered can be in many different forms and of many different types and may cover the consumer, the competition, the market and the wider economy. It may look at what has been happening in the past or it may try to look into the future. It allows businesses to understand consumer behaviour and to make decisions that make them more responsive to customers' needs and to increase profits.

Market research helps to give a business a competitive advantage by improving its products and services and to successfully market them. It is crucial for any business start-up to reduce the risks involved, and is also essential for established businesses to keep up with market trends and remain competitive. Market research can provide information about potential gaps in the market and their potential for growth.

> **Market research** is any kind of activity that gives a business information about its product or service, its customers, its competitors or the market it operates in.

Product and market orientation

Product and market orientation refers to where a business focuses its priorities. Product orientation means that a business concentrates on the production process and the product itself. Product orientated businesses place their efforts into creating and developing a technically impressive product and then trying to sell it to the consumer. This approach was much more common in 'the old days' although a number of businesses still do this now. This is particularly true for technologically innovative products. Steve Jobs of Apple famously said "A lot of times, people don't know what they want until you show it to them."

Market orientation is when a business concentrates on the wants of the consumer and is led by the market. By focusing on the wants and needs of the customer the business is much more likely to produce a product or service that the customer wants and will therefore buy. This will give that business a competitive advantage over rival businesses, which may not be so closely focused on the customer. If the customer is kept satisfied by the business, then brand loyalty may be created and the customer is more likely to purchase more products or services from the business.

Figure 2.1: Product and market orientation

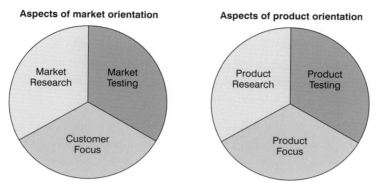

Aspects of market orientation

Market Research | Market Testing | Customer Focus

Aspects of product orientation

Product Research | Product Testing | Product Focus

Activity

Identify three products that you think are likely to be product orientated and three that are likely to be market orientated. Explain why you have chosen them.

Primary and Secondary research

Market research falls into two main categories, Primary and Secondary research.

> **Primary research** – The gathering of information first hand from an original source that has not been collected before. Often involves asking people for specific information hence its alternative name **Field research**. Examples include questionnaires, focus groups and direct interviews. Direct observation is important too, especially for small businesses, it may help in deciding where to locate, for example.
>
> **Secondary research** – Finding and using information that has already been gathered by somebody else. Sometimes called **Desk research**, as it can be done by reading books and journals, but increasingly using online information. Google, trade journals and National Statistics are examples.

Market research can be either primary or secondary.

Primary research has the advantage that it can be designed for the exact needs of the business. The information that is produced will be relevant and up to date and only available to the business, not to its competitors. On the other hand, this is likely to be expensive, especially if an outside agency is conducting the research. It may also take a long time to collect, and great care must be taken with the wording of questions and methods of sampling to avoid inaccuracies or errors.

Secondary research is information that already exists and has already been collected by someone else. It can be easy to access online and can be cheap or free. However, it may not be exactly what the business is looking for as it has been collected for a different purpose. It may also be out of date and its accuracy is not always known, particularly if it is found online.

A combination of both types of research is usually most effective. Secondary research can be used to get an overall picture of the market or situation and then primary research can be used to fill in any gaps or answer specific questions.

	Primary research	**Secondary research**
Advantages	<ul><li>Is up to date as it is conducted as required.</li><li>Can be tailored to the precise needs of the business.</li><li>Can produce data which rivals do not have access to.</li></ul>	<ul><li>Is available immediately and often relatively inexpensively (or free), normally cheaper than primary research from scratch.</li></ul>
Disadvantages	<ul><li>Can be expensive.</li><li>Can be time consuming to collect and interpret data.</li><li>Methods such as focus groups can require specialist skills.</li></ul>	<ul><li>May be out of date.</li><li>Difficult to guarantee accuracy.</li><li>Can be expensive to purchase (e.g. market reports).</li><li>Rivals can access this data too.</li></ul>

The Houdini Stop

The Houdini story started four years ago when Bianca Richardson, desperate to stop her two-year-old daughter wriggling out of her car seat, came up with a device called the Houdini Stop involving webbing and bracer clips.

It worked very well and she was soon supplying them to friends. She then started serious market research to see if it would work as a business. She also had the device tested, to make sure it worked on all types of car seats, would not hinder the seat performance and was not a choking hazard.

Houdini Stop passed the testing and took off. She has sold about 60,000 devices so far in New Zealand and Australia. Her market now includes Britain, Ireland, Poland, Spain and she is working on entering the Brazilian market. Bianca has since invented another two products, Houdini Locks and Houdini Cosys. The locks keep disposable nappies on and the Cosys keep cot blankets in place.

Questions

1. Explain how Bianca might have used both primary and secondary research in developing her products.

2. Explain any possible drawbacks to this research.

Quantitative and Qualitative research

> **Quantitative research** is based on numerical data, measures things and produces statistical information e.g. the number of times 18 to 25 year olds go to the cinema or the percentage of Toyota's sales now made in China. The main types of quantitative research are sampling and questionnaires.
>
> **Qualitative research** is based on feelings, attitudes and opinions. It tries to identify why consumers behave the way they do e.g. how they react to a new product, how does the customer feel when buying chocolate. The main types of qualitative research are focus groups and interviews.

Quantitative research produces data on market size and buyers' other characteristics such as age, gender and location. Qualitative research goes deeper and produces information on how customers feel about the product. In both cases, strategies for gathering information are changing.

There are far fewer face-to-face interviews than there used to be, as researchers use the telephone or the internet to gather information. Supermarkets keep in close touch with customers using their loyalty cards. These approaches cut the cost of research. However, many businesses still give great weight to designers' judgements about what is likely to succeed. The best example of this approach is Apple, which has repeatedly developed new and very successful products, based on creativity and innovation.

Limitations of market research, sample size and bias

Whilst market research does reduce the risks of failure, many new products and ideas still fail despite its use. Estimates of the failure rate of new products and services vary. The University of Toronto found the failure rate for new products launched in the US grocery sector to be 70 to 80%. Not just new start-ups or inexperienced businesses get it wrong. Think about Microsoft Vista or Coca-Cola's New Coke, both failed to understand the needs of the market despite having undertaken research.

Failing to ask the right questions is common. Discovering how often consumers use a particular gym may be useful but it may be of more use to find out why they don't use it more. In the mid-1990s British Airways asked business fliers what they wanted and they said good food and wine, comfortable seats, more video choices and personal screens. Very few mentioned data sockets on satellite phones and power supplies in arm rests so they could use PCs. This turned out to be a costly error as BA's rivals such as American Airlines and Lufthansa had picked up on the need for this. BA lost sales and had to pay to retrofit the technology.

It is impossible to ask the whole market what they think, so a sample is taken. This can be tricky to get right. It has to be representative of the whole market or errors will creep in. A survey conducted at 10 o'clock in the morning in the high street would not be representative as many people would be at work and their views would not be collected. Too small a sample and it might be unrepresentative, too big and it may be too costly and time consuming. Samples should also be relevant. For Bianca Richardson in the case study above this would have meant researching views of parents with young children. Surveying the whole population would have been wasteful and unhelpful.

"Now give us your spontaneous response"

Some businesses just sample their existing customers. This can lead to bias as they are probably already favourable towards the business and its brand. It may be more useful to survey people who don't currently buy that brand. Care must be taken with questions; they should not lead the participant towards a particular response. In focus groups, where groups discuss issues, some people tend to be more vocal than others – giving a misleading impression. There are many areas where bias can creep in but it would take a whole book to do justice to them.

BA found that market research has its limits.

Use of ICT to support market research

There is no doubt that ICT can be a useful market research tool. The click of the mouse can reveal a wealth of information for secondary research. The problem is not finding the information but narrowing the choice down to get helpful results. ICT can also be used in primary research, in the form of online surveys and questionnaires. Platforms such as Facebook and Twitter provide businesses with a way of getting valuable feedback from customers, not only a way of promoting their business. The danger here is that the sample of people responding will not be representative so bias will be present.

ICT can also be used in exploring databases. This process of 'data mining' is secondary research. Many businesses hold vast quantities of data on their customers. Amazon holds the records of every purchase by every customer. From this they can analyse buying patterns and trends on a national and individual level. This is how they tailor their marketing specifically to individuals and small groups with shared interests. Supermarkets use their loyalty cards to accumulate information about their customers as well; they will also track customers by their use of debit and credit cards.

Businesses often supplement their own customer data with data from other sources, such as the electoral roll, Land Registry, the Office for National Statistics and credit reports. Understanding the demographics of the general population provides useful information when making large operational decisions such as deciding on new products, advertising and business location. Tesco collected so much information that they now own the Crucible data base, which sells that data to other businesses.

Activity

Use an online search for Experianplc.com to learn a little about what they offer.

Market segmentation

A market contains many different types of customer; it is unlikely that one product will satisfy all consumers in the market. For example one magazine is unlikely to appeal to both sexes, old and young. Markets are therefore split up into groups of consumers that have similar wants and needs. One group of consumers is the target market, identified as a market segment.

> **Market segmentation** means dividing the market into groups of consumers with similar characteristics. Common groupings include; age, gender, income, interests, location. This enables products and services to be more effectively targeted at a particular segment.

Some segments are very large and general, e.g. *Radio Times* magazine is just aimed at anyone who watches television whereas *Vintage Tractors* magazine is clearly aimed at a small group of people with a common interest in the subject.

Alternatively, markets may be segmented by product. For example, buyers of 4-wheel drive vehicles constitute one segment of the car market. Or a market may be segmented according to the level of luxury involved, as with clothing. An important difference is that a segment is a sub-section of a larger market whereas a market niche is more of a separate market.

Products for segmented markets	Markets segmented by
Package holidays e.g. cheap beach holidays, safaris, exotic locations.	Age, income, interests.
TV stations, e.g. ITV1, BBC4, Sky 1.	Age, education, hobbies.
Housing – starter homes, flats, houses.	Income, location, family size.

Some researchers segment the market in 4 main ways…

Geographical by area	Demographic by type of person	Behavioural by usage	Psychographic by attitudes
Area	Age	Occasions	Lifestyle
County	Gender	Frequency	Social class
Region	Occupation	Loyalty	Values
City	Income	Usage	Attitudes
Rural	Religion	Benefits	Opinions
Country	Race		

Segmentation is useful for a business as it more precisely identifies the consumer. The more precisely a segment can be identified and provided for, the more likely it is that a sale will be made. This also reduces direct competition and can mean that a premium (higher) price may be charged when market segments get exactly what they want. If they do, then brand loyalty is created which means repeat purchases are likely and word of mouth will attract new customers.

Segmentation is not always straightforward. The process of researching and identifying different segments can be costly and time consuming. It is more costly to develop and market separate variants for different segments rather than just one standardised product. By targeting one particular segment it may mean ignoring others. Even if segments are identified it may not be easy to reach them.

Catering for the needs of small market segments may raise costs and prices. Standardised products with a mass market cost less to produce. But if customers value the products that are designed to suit them the best, they will be prepared to pay a bit more to get exactly what they want.

Chapter 3

Market positioning

Discussion point

Why is it useful for a product to stand out?

Market positioning: market mapping and market maps

> **Market positioning** is how individual products or brands are seen in relation to their competition by consumers. This may stem from pricing, marketing or perceived quality.

Market positioning concerns how the business places its products in the minds of consumers, in relation to competing products. Businesses need to decide if they want to follow the competition with a similar product or whether they want to create a 'different' image for their product. A business that has found a gap in the market can differentiate its product so as to target that gap.

Positioning the product in the right place can be very beneficial. It may be best to be close to the market leader, e.g. the new generation of phones mimicking the iPhone. Or it may be possible to go to a part of the market that is yet to be catered for, as Dyson did with the original bagless vacuum cleaners. A distinctive product is more likely to secure some degree of customer loyalty.

Businesses with long-existing products may decide to re-position them in the market. In the 1990s, the image of Skoda cars was so poor that they were the subject of jokes. Skoda retained its market position in the minds of customers as a very competitively priced car, but successfully re-positioned itself by improving reliability and so becoming an award winning car manufacturer. Customer perceptions shifted to regard the cars as generally better quality and value for money.

In some cases businesses have re-positioned themselves from one segment to another. The best example is Lucozade, which moved from being a health drink to aid recovery from illness, to a best-selling, trendy sports drink for athletes! There was no change in the product initially, but advertising subtly changed customer perceptions about its possible uses.

Market mapping

> **Market mapping** is the use of a grid showing two features of a market, such as price and consumer age. Individual brands or businesses are added to the grid to identify potential niches or gaps in the market. It also helps to position products in relation to each other.

Market mapping is a useful visual tool to see at a glance where different products or brands lie in relation to each other. The axes can vary and may plot a range of variables against each other such as speed against fuel economy or comfort against aerodynamics (in the case of cars). A market map for performance cars might plot comfort to power against elegance to technical design. A market map for soft drinks might plot low to high sugar against low to high carbonation. Other variables that could be contrasted include:

Feature	
High quality v. basic quality	Male v. female
Mass v. niche market	Old v. young
Modern v. traditional	Urban customers v. rural customers
Aesthetic v. functional	High income customers v. low income customers
Luxury v. value	Complex technology v. simple

Figure 3.1: A simplified market map

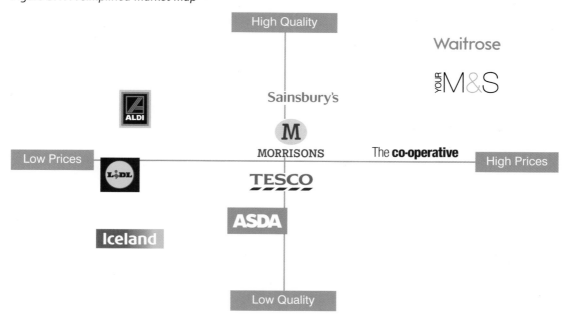

Mapping reveals any potential gaps in the market. However, identifying a gap does not mean there is a need for a product to fill it. Careful market research will need to be done to see if it is viable or not. As someone once said *"Just because there is a gap in the market, it does not mean there is a market in the gap."* In the example above it is unlikely that there will be a market for expensive low quality cars, but there may be an opportunity for a high quality less expensive car if production costs allow. Market mapping can also help a business to differentiate its product from the competition, in order to attract sales.

Competitive advantage of a product or service

> **Competitive advantage** is any feature of a business that enables it to compete effectively with rival products. An advantage may be based on price, quality, service, reputation or innovation. A convenient location may be significant. Product differentiation may be used to achieve an advantage.

In competitive markets, businesses strive for competitive advantage in order to avoid falling sales and rising losses. There are many different ways that a business can achieve an advantage. Cutting costs can allow a business to compete on price. Investment in new production technologies or improving relationships with suppliers may cut costs. New technologies can also create opportunities to improve product design or introduce completely new products. Improvements in staff training may lead to improved product reliability or customer service.

Businesses that enhance their competitive advantages by cutting prices or adding value (see below) to the product are likely to be able to sell more and sometimes raise prices too. It helps to reduce competition if consumers see something a little different about the product or service. Perceived good value for money may be based on a low price e.g. Aldi or a reputation for quality e.g. Skoda. A brand image may become associated with technical excellence or appealing design features e.g. Apple. Competitive advantage applies to services as well as manufactures. It is easy to see how better staff training might improve the services offered in a hotel or a fitness centre.

Figure 3.2: Competitive advantage

Lower price

Customer service

Higher quality

Reliability

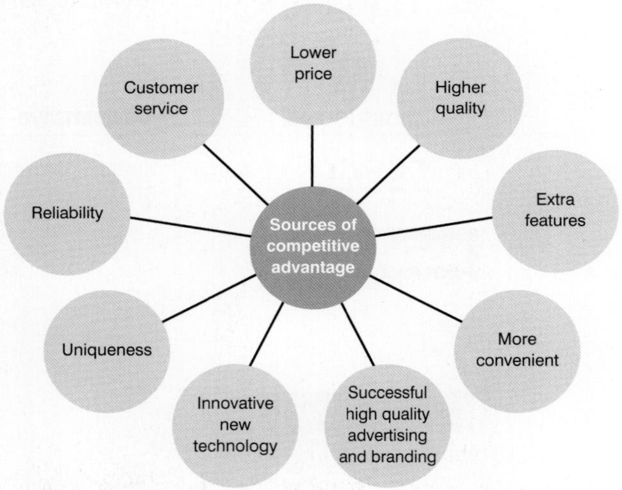

Sources of competitive advantage

Extra features

Uniqueness

More convenient

Innovative new technology

Successful high quality advertising and branding

Product differentiation

Competitive advantage can be enhanced by making a product or service different to the competition. The difference may be real or imaginary; it does not matter as long as the consumer perceives it to be different. The whole purpose of branding and promotion is to create product differentiation. There is very little physical difference between different t-shirts but a little bit of print with the right name or logo can significantly increase the asking price.

> **Product differentiation** occurs when businesses make their product distinct from rival products. This may involve giving it unique features to attract customers, or it may involve changing perceptions as to the function or image of the product.

Product differentiation and competitive advantage are less relevant to commodity products where everyone is selling the same thing. However, there is a grey area here. Unleaded petrol has to conform to strict regulations and must have a set quality. Businesses still build brand images in attempts to make their brand of fuel seem different and somehow 'better'.

A distinctive and attractive differentiating feature can become a **unique selling point** (**USP**). Marketing can stress the value of the feature to reinforce a superior image to consumers. Sky Sports, for example, uses showing the most live premiership soccer games as a USP. Their determination to maintain this USP helps to explain why UK premiership broadcast rights for 2016-19 sold for more than £5bn. Where exclusivity is hard to protect, a strong USP is soon copied and becomes standard. Think, for example, of adding features such as GPS positioning technology to smartphones.

> A **unique selling point** (or unique selling proposition) is an attractive feature or benefit associated with one particular brand alone.

By achieving product differentiation the business has created an image or product that consumers will recognise and hopefully want to buy. Brand loyalty is created and this can be built on to ensure repeat purchases and future sales. It can also enable the business to charge a higher price, the more distinctive a product becomes then the fewer substitutes there are in the mind of the consumer. As a result they are more likely to buy the product even if price is relatively high.

Activity

Choose four businesses that sell similar products with which you are familiar and explain how each one differentiates itself from the others, e.g. **casual clothing** – *Jack Wills, Superdry, Abercrombie & Fitch* and *Hollister*; **Supermarkets** – *Sainsbury's, Waitrose, Aldi* and *Morrisons*.

Adding value to products/services

In order to make a profit a business needs more revenue than costs. It needs to turn its factor inputs into something that will sell for more than its costs. This process is called **adding value**. It is the reward for turning inputs into something for which consumers have effective demand at a profitable price. One aspect of this is efficient use of inputs to control costs. The converse side of ensuring the desirability of products to consumers is often given more attention. Using expensive inputs is fine if the return on them outweighs the cost.

Adding value is easy to understand with physical products where parts are put together to make something useful. A chair is a simple example. The chef in the restaurant adds value by preparing and cooking ingredients to

A chef adds value by cooking ingredients to produce a meal.

produce a meal. Customers in the restaurant then pay much more than the cost of the ingredients because of the added value. The restaurant adds further value by providing nice surroundings, attentive service and doing the washing up!

Understanding added value in service industries takes a little more thought. McDonalds adds value by its speedy and convenient service and drive through facility. Many retailers add value by making things available in the right place at the right time. Florists add value by carefully wrapping flowers in attractive papers and ribbons. Holiday companies add value by providing all inclusive holidays.

Value is essentially about consumer perception of 'worth'. An iPhone 6 is worth more than £500 to many consumers. A successfully differentiated product with competitive advantage in a profitable market segment can be expected to have added value. Apple had a 40% profit margin on iPhones and made a record £12bn profit in its last quarter of 2014.

> **Added value** is the difference between the price paid and the total cost of the inputs needed to create a product. Goods and services must add value to be profitable.

Exam style question

iPhone X

Apple has introduced 18 models of iPhone since it was first launched in 2007. There are estimated to be 700 million iPhones in use worldwide. The iPhone X reached many countries in 2017. It had an edge to edge screen, no home button, facial ID and a 5.8 inch retina display. The Apple brand has become strongly differentiated by up to the minute design.

In the last quarter of 2017, Apple reported revenue of $88.3bn (£61.9bn), compared to $78.4bn (£55bn) in the same quarter of the previous year. The results also revealed a record quarterly profit of $20.1bn (£14bn).

Rivals have worked hard and spent heavily to duplicate the appeal of Apple products. Apple and leading rival Samsung were involved in long running court cases over patents (exclusive rights to features or products). Component suppliers have had warnings from Apple that leaking any details of new products will end their contracts and bring claims for damages.

Other suppliers in this dynamic market have cheaper phones and phones with advantages on various individual features. In total, Android phones outsell those using Apple's iOS several times over. However, other firms fall way behind Apple's profitability.

Questions

1. What is meant by differentiation?	(2 marks)
2. What is meant by dynamic market?	(2 marks)
3. Explain market positioning in the context of mobile phones.	(4 marks)
4. Briefly explain two reasons for Apple regularly introducing new iPhones.	(4 marks)
5. To what extent is market research important to a business such as Apple?	(8 marks)
6. Evaluate reasons for Apple's competitive advantage.	(10 marks)

Chapter 4
Demand

Figure 4.1: An inverse relationship

When P ↑	Q ↓
When P ↓	Q ↑

Discussion point

Why does a higher price generally lead to lower sales?

In the previous unit we looked at the market in general and talked about buyers and sellers. This unit goes into more detail about how buyers decide the demand for a product or service. The interaction between demand and supply determines both price and quantity and also decides what gets produced. Buyers create demand and in response producers create supply.

> **Demand** – the amount of a good or service that people are willing and able to buy at a given price, at a given time.

Market demand refers to the sum of all individual demands for a particular good or service. (Note that demand has to be *effective*; it is no good just to *want* something. Consumers must be able to pay for it at that price, there and then.)

There is a relationship between price and quantity demanded. This is usually an inverse relationship: as one changes the other moves in the opposite direction. As **price (P)** rises, **quantity (Q)** falls and vice versa.

Factors leading to a change in demand

A number of factors will alter the level of demand at any given price and cause people to buy either more or less of something. *This is caused by a change in a factor other than price.* For some reason people want to buy *more* or *less* of it than before even though the price is the *same*.

Changes in the prices of other goods – If prices of *related* goods change, the quantity demanded of the original good can change as well.

1. **Substitutes** are goods that can be consumed in place of one another. If the price of a substitute increases, the demand for the original good increases. e.g. if the price of Nescafé increases, the demand for Kenco coffee will increase as consumers switch to the now comparatively cheaper substitute.

2. **Complements** are goods that are normally consumed together such as cars and petrol, the purchase of one will lead to the purchase of the complementary good as well. If the price of a complement increases, consumers respond by buying less of it and so the demand for the other complementary good decreases. If the price of a complement decreases, the demand for the other complementary good increases. If, for example, the price of computers falls, then the demand for computer software increases.

Changes in consumer incomes – As incomes change so does the quantity demanded. For most goods and services as income rises so too does the quantity demanded. As income drops, so does quantity; these are called **normal goods**.

Some goods and services work the other way round. As income increases quantity demanded falls and as income falls demand increases. These are called **inferior goods**.

Examples of inferior goods are usually cheaper substitutes. As incomes fall consumers switch to cheaper products to save money and demand for them increases despite the fall in income. As incomes rise consumers switch back to the more expensive variety. Examples include public transport and supermarket's own brand budget ranges.

Fashions, tastes and preferences – The consumer's demand for products and services changes all the time, fashions and fads come and go. If the preference for a particular product increases, then the demand for that product will also increase. If something is no longer seen as desirable then demand will fall. At the time of writing Twitter is declining in popularity and has been overtaken by Instagram. On a more long term trend the demand for vegetarian options has been increasing steadily as more people become more health conscious and decide not to eat meat.

Advertising and branding – The whole point of advertising is to make us all buy more of something i.e. to increase the quantity demanded. Branding works in a similar way, the strength of the brand helps to persuade consumers to buy more of the product and increase demand. This is closely linked to the previous section on fashions and tastes.

What advertising and branding is really doing is persuading us that there are few if any acceptable substitutes and that we must buy this particular brand and therefore increase its demand. It will also create consumer loyalty and encourage repeat purchases.

Demographics – Refers to the structure and characteristics of the population. In a general sense it means that as populations grow then so too will the demand for most goods and services. It can also mean specific changes within the population. At the moment there has been an increase in the number of young children in the UK which creates extra demand for childcare and primary school places. In a few years' time this bulge in our population will increase the demand for products aimed at teenagers and so on. There are currently 10 million people in the UK over 65 years old. The latest projections are for 5½ million more elderly people in 20 years' time and the number will have nearly doubled to around 19 million by 2050.

External shocks – Refer to the impact a sudden change can bring to demand for a product or service. They can be external and extreme, for example the 9/11 attacks in America had a profound impact on demand for air travel. Just prior to this, US airlines boarded 56.3 million passengers a year for domestic service; after the terrorist attack it took three years for demand to once again reach the 56 million mark. It can also be internal, for example an increase in tax is likely to cause a fall in demand for most goods as this effectively reduces the income consumers are able to spend.

Seasonality – The time of year or even day can affect demand. Think of Easter eggs, fireworks and winter coats, or the demand for electricity as the kettles go on during the ad breaks for Coronation Street! In addition the weather and climate can have a big impact. The demand for ice cream is likely to be higher on a hot sunny day in August than a cloudy one.

Focus on price

Price plays a key role in deciding what people choose to buy. A higher price means we give up more alternatives in order to have something. At a lower price, we give up less so the product should become better value for money and more attractive. This means that the amount demanded should increase. Just think of how much busier shops are during the sales and on 'Black Friday'. There is normally an inverse relationship between price and quantity demanded. When we need to analyse markets we use **demand schedules** and **demand curves** to show this basic relationship.

A demand schedule is just a listing and a demand curve is simply a graphical illustration [a picture] of the link between the price charged and the level of demand. The convention is to show the price level on the vertical axis and quantity on the horizontal axis, with zero for both scales at the bottom left of the diagram. The curve should slope downwards from left to right, and even though we call it a curve we often draw it as a simple straight line.

Figure 4.2: Demand curve and schedule

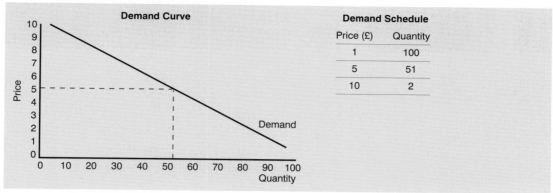

It is important to understand and remember that any demand curve focuses on price and assumes that none of the other influences on demand changes. A change in any of the other relevant factors will cause a shift to a new demand curve. A change which increases demand will move the curve to the right. If demand falls, the curve shifts left. The whole point of the demand curve is to show the relationship with price. A rise in price will cause a movement up and left along the existing demand curve (called a contraction of demand). A fall in price causes a movement down and right along it (an extension of demand).

⚠ WATCH OUT!

Muddled students get tangled between a movement along a demand curve – when price changes – and a shift to a new demand curve (when any other determinant changes). Stay clear on this.

Figure 4.3: Changes in demand

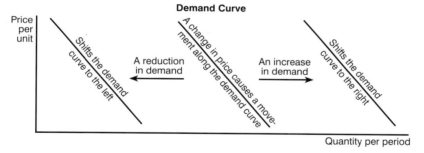

Demand schedule – a table showing the quantities demanded at different price levels.

Demand curve – a graphical representation of the relationship between quantity demanded and price, for a product in a market.

Contraction of demand – move up and left on a demand curve when price rises.

Extension of demand – move down and right on a demand curve when price falls.

Try this

1. Starting from the mental image of a cinema near you, make a rough estimate of how many customers would buy tickets this evening at £3, £5, £10 and £20 each.

2. Convert this information into a demand curve.

3. If the current price is £5, show the quantity of tickets sold at that price.

4. On your diagram, illustrate what happens (i) if the price rises to £7, (ii) or if bad weather closes down local public transport and makes roads dangerous, (iii) or if full time students in the area have all just received payment of a new type of maintenance grant.

Chapter 5

Supply

Milk production

Higher milk prices during 2013 stimulated production in the UK and globally. In the first half of 2014, EU milk production was up 5%, New Zealand up 8.4%, USA up 1.4% and UK production for January to November 2014 was 9% up on 2013. With continued good weather and plentiful forage supplies, there is no sign on the horizon of milk supply falling in the short term.

Consecutive months of high domestic milk production over the past year have led to an abundance of supply. High domestic production, combined with the ban on dairy imports to Russia and falling returns from global markets, have resulted in a fall in milk prices. UK farmers operate in a global dairy market. Their exports account for a small percentage of milk produced, but have a major impact on price. Most UK milk processors have reduced their payments to farmers for raw liquid milk. Further price falls have been publicly announced by several large processors for the coming months.

Discussion points

1. Why was the supply of milk higher in 2014 than earlier?
2. How might farmers react to falling milk prices?

Businesses pay the costs of inputs such as labour and materials in order to produce their output and gain revenue from selling it. Decisions on the amount to produce will be based on their cost structure and the amount of revenue and profit they are likely to make. Our starting assumption is that businesses want to maximise profit, so the amount they produce and supply to the market will be decided by what they see as most profitable.

> **Supply** – the amount of a good or service that producers are willing and able to market, at a given price, at a given period of time.

Market supply refers to the sum of all individual supplies of a particular good or service. (Note that supply has to be *effective*; it is no good just being *willing* to supply something. producers must actually be able to supply it at that price, there and then.)

We assume that unit costs generally rise as output increases, perhaps because some workers are then paid at overtime rates or some other cost rises faster than output. Profit seeking businesses will produce and sell whilst extra costs are below the revenue from selling extra products made. If increasing output means that costs rise more than revenue, there is no profit to be made from making and selling more.

A higher price increases revenue and normally gives producers an incentive to supply more. Even if their costs increase when producing more, a higher price increases revenue from sales. If the revenue increase is greater than the cost increase for extra output, profits will rise. This is the incentive which attracts extra supply. The fashion for selfie photos created a market for extra kit. The first selfie sticks (in Asia) sold well and prices rose. This led the makers to increase output. More sticks were supplied at a high price.

Figure 5.1: The effect of price changes on supply

When P ↑	Q ↑
When P ↓	Q ↓

Supply curves normally slope upwards from left to right, showing that less will be supplied at a low price and more at a high price. North Sea Oil producers drill in deep waters and have relatively high costs, but these were more than covered when the oil prices were around $110 per barrel in mid-2014. In the winter of 2014-15, prices fell to below $50 per barrel. British Petroleum (BP) and other producers reacted by reducing North Sea production. They supplied less at a lower price. Oil prices are eventually likely to rise again. When this happens, North Sea producers will probably respond by once again increasing their output.

Figure 5.2: The supply curve

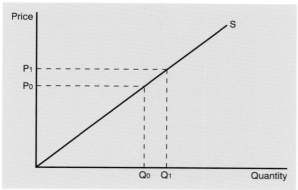

If price goes up from P_0 to P_1, quantity increases from Q_0 to Q_1.

> A **supply curve** is a graphical representation of the relationship between quantity supplied and price, for a product in a market. As with demand, the 'curve' is often shown as a straight line.

The positive relationship between price and quantity supplied is the opposite of demand (where the relationship is negative and the curve slopes the other way). Both supply and demand curves focus just on the influence of price on quantity, ignoring or freezing other possible influences. Figures 5.1 and 5.2 show the effects of a change in price on the quantity supplied.

Try this

In February 2014 North Sea Oil sold at $100 per barrel and production was 850,000 barrels. A year later, at a price of $50 per barrel, some high cost oilfields were temporarily closed and production fell to 650,000 barrels (all data rounded). Assume that there was no other change in conditions of supply, and that output at $75 per barrel would be 750,000 barrels. Turn this information into a supply curve.

The long run

A supply curve refers to a specific market and a limited period of time. In the longer term more changes become possible. For example, the profitability of selfie sticks in Asia attracted new producers. After the time it took them to organise machinery and production, market supply increased – shifting the supply curve as shown in Figure 5.3. This longer term shift is likely to lead to a lower price and reduced profitability. Eventually, price and output are likely to settle at a steadier level.

The distinction here is that some changes to output can be made cheaply and quickly, such as buying more materials and asking workers to put in longer hours. We refer to the time period involved here as the **short run**. Adding to machinery and constructing buildings are examples of **long run** changes. The time periods involved are not precise and vary between industries. For example, building new nuclear power plant takes far longer than leasing and equipping a new tattoo parlour.

In supply theory, the **short run** is the time period in which at least one component in production cannot be changed.

The **long run** is the time period in which all productive assets can be changed.

Most supply curves show how quantity supplied will react to price changes in the short run. The bigger changes in output which become possible in the long run are shown by shifting the supply curve rather than a movement along it. A long run increase in supply will shift the supply curve outwards to the right. A long run contraction as an industry shrinks will shift the supply curve inwards and left.

Figure 5.3: Shifting the supply curve

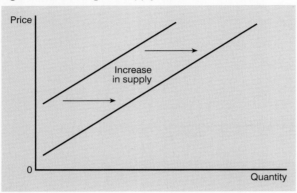

Other factors influencing supply

Price is not the only variable that can lead to a change in supply. There are a number of other factors that will alter the amount supplied at any given price. The price of the product has not changed but for some reason producers want to supply *more* or *less* of it than before, even though the price is the *same*. In a dynamic market, supply curves can shift frequently. Several of these other determinants of supply are explained below:

Changes in the costs of production – An increase in costs directly affects the amount a producer is willing to supply. If a furniture maker has to pay more for wood, then profits decline. The reduced profitability may mean the producer supplies less furniture at the lower price. If costs decline, producers respond by increasing output. The furniture manufacturer may increase production if wood costs fall because profits will increase at that price.

The introduction of new technology – Changes in technology are a very important reason why costs may fall in many activities. New technology nearly always means an improvement of some kind and greater efficiency. Technological progress allows firms to produce a given item at a lower average cost. Computer controlled machinery may be faster and more accurate, resulting in lower cost per unit of output. As a result more may be supplied at the same price.

Computer controlled machinery may result in lower cost per unit of output

Indirect taxes – When the government intervenes in a market it may be because it wants to tax a product to cut consumption or to raise revenue (as with petrol). A tax on a product in addition to the costs for the producer, or an increase in a tax, causes a fall in supply. Adding an indirect tax onto a supply curve shifts it vertically upwards.

Government subsidies – Subsidies are payments to producers to encourage production and will increase supply. The subsidy cuts the cost of production for the producer so they are therefore willing and able to supply more at each and every price. A current example would be the range of subsidies available to individuals and businesses to create green energy from wind and solar power.

External shocks – The supply of some goods is dependent on events beyond the producer's control. This covers both sudden and unexpected events such as the Japanese tsunami that adversely affected the supply of many Japanese products such as Toyota cars. It also includes variations in natural phenomena such as climatic changes which can affect the amount of a crop that is harvested. A wet summer is likely to mean that the supply of wheat will be less after a poor harvest. Flooding in Somerset in the winter of 2013-14 stopped the supply of milk from dairy farms which were under water and/or inaccessible.

A change in any factor influencing supply, other than price, leads to a shift to a new supply curve. Anything which leads to a decrease in supply shifts the curve inwards and left, any increase shifts the supply curve outwards and right.

Figure 5.4: Increases and decreases in supply

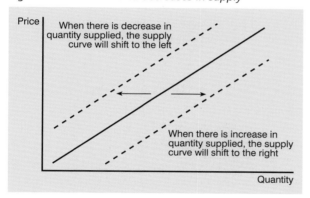

> ## ⚠ WATCH OUT!
>
> Shifting a supply curve inwards and left looks intuitively like an increase, but is not. This is a decrease as less will now be supplied at any price. Check this and try to learn it. Many students struggle on this point.

Try this

Starting from the image of a normal supply curve, which way will it shift if (i) workers have a wage increase, and (ii) computer aided design brings greater speed and efficiency?

Why are indirect taxes and subsidies likely to move a supply curve up or down rather than left or right?

Chapter 6

Markets

Have any D-I-Y stores closed in your area? If so, what has happened to their buildings?

The interaction of supply and demand

Markets are formed where sellers and buyers interact. The combination of supply and demand forms the basis of market activity. When supply and demand curves intersect they identify the price at which the amount consumers want to buy in a time period is the same as the producers are willing to supply. This is called the **equilibrium price** and can be shown on a diagram using demand and supply curves.

The intersection also shows the equilibrium quantity. There will be no unsold stocks and customers will be able to buy all they demand at that price. This is known as **market clearing**. Figure 6.1 shows an example with an equilibrium price of £50 and quantity of 400. Total revenue will be price x quantity, so £20,000 here.

Figure 6.1: Equilibrium price and quantity

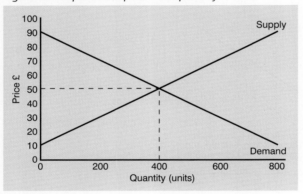

How to get the demand and supply curves the right way round
Every year some exam candidates get their curves mixed up. Remember them this way...

Demand starts with a **D** – the Demand curve slopes **DOWN** from L to R.

s**UP**ply has the word **UP** in it – the Supply curve slopes **UP** from L to R.

⚠ WATCH OUT!

Always label the axes and curves on a diagram. Failure to do this is penalised by examiners.

If the price was above the equilibrium then more would be supplied than demanded, this would result in a surplus of unwanted products. The way to clear a surplus is to reduce the price. As a result of a lower price more is demanded and less supplied, shifting the market back towards equilibrium. If price is below equilibrium then more will be demanded than supplied, this time there is a shortage of product and so price rises, less is demanded and more is supplied until the equilibrium price is restored.

> **Equilibrium price** – the price at which quantity supplied and quantity demanded are equal in a market, leaving neither excess supply nor excess demand.

> **Market clearing** – obtaining a balance between quantity supplied and quantity demanded, normally by arriving at the equilibrium price.

If businesses supply more than consumers will buy at a price, there is excess supply. When demand exceeds supply at the current price, there is excess demand.

Figure 6.2: Excess supply, excess demand and market clearing

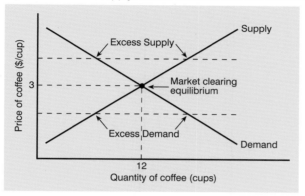

At a price above $3 per cup the supply of coffee will exceed demand, price should fall. At a price below $3 there is excess demand so price should rise.

Supply and demand diagrams to show the causes and consequences of price changes

In a static market where nothing much changes, a market equilibrium price and quantity could be long lasting. In dynamic markets prices change frequently. Think, for example, of the stock exchange where company share prices often fluctuate throughout a day. Any change in the factors influencing demand or supply will disrupt equilibrium by shifting one of the curves. When something changes, we should first identify whether demand or supply is involved and then whether there is an increase or a fall.

A change in the factors of demand will shift the demand curve to the right if demand increases or to the left if demand falls, as shown below:

Figure 6.3: Changes in demand

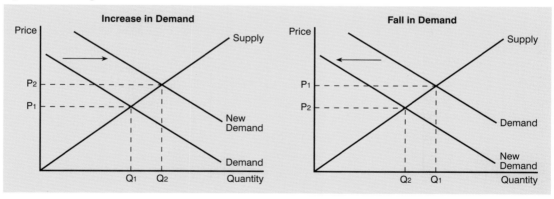

The increase in demand shows the demand curve shifting to the right as more will be wanted at any price. This could be due to a change in tastes, for example. At the previous price there would now be excess demand. With an upward sloping supply curve, this shift in demand will mean moving up the supply curve to a higher price and an increased quantity at the new equilibrium (P2, Q2). A fall in demand (perhaps caused by a fall in income) shifts the demand curve to the left; there would be excess supply at the previous price. Both price and quantity will fall if the supply curve has the normal slope.

If there is a change in one of the determinants of supply, the supply curve will shift and there will be a movement along the demand curve.

Technological progress could cause a fall in costs and an increase in supply. There would now be excess supply at P1 so a shift to P2 is likely, with an increase in quantity and a fall in price. Shortage of materials and a rise in their cost could cause a fall in supply. There would be excess demand at P1, price is likely to rise. On a normal demand curve this will also bring a fall in the equilibrium quantity from Q1 to Q2.

Figure 6.4: Changes in supply

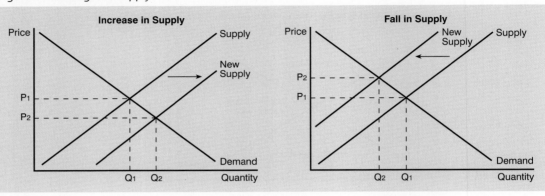

Sample scenario – The market for ski equipment in summer

Step 1 – Draw a basic D&S diagram

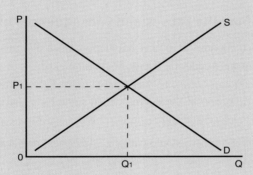

Step 2 – Decide which curve(s) is/are affected and add to diagram

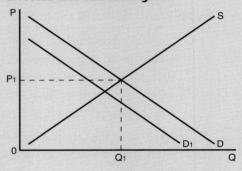

Step 3 – Show new equilibrium price and quantity

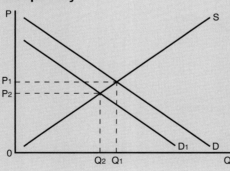

Step 4 – Provide a written explanation

Consumers are less likely to want to buy ski equipment in the summer as it is not the ski season and they may prefer to spend their money on summer holidays and other purchases. As a result the demand curve shifts to the left and less is sold.

Activity

Draw a demand and supply diagram for each of the following situations. Explain what is happening.

1. The market for bread following an increase in the price of flour.
2. The market for Daz washing powder following an increase in the price of Ariel washing powder.
3. The market for foreign holidays following an increase in income tax.
4. The market for apples following a fine autumn and a record harvest.

The implications of market forces (demand and supply) for businesses are very important. Rising prices may indicate increasing demand. Managers who understand their market may realise that they can safely increase output and perhaps also raise prices, so increasing their profits substantially.

On the other hand demand may be falling and orders diminishing. A price cut may arrest the slide but more likely, the business will need to cut output before it starts to make significant losses. To stay alive it may have to come up with a new and more popular product. If a fall in demand is sustained, businesses are likely to leave the industry. This is the **profit signalling mechanism** giving firms indicators which can guide their actions.

Do-it-yourself maintenance and house improvements have had a fall in demand. D-I-Y stores have become less profitable. Some have closed and their premises have been transferred to more profitable alternative uses. Such a fall in demand could be shown as the shift from D to D1 on Figure 6.5 . Initially, a short term shift down and left on supply curve S would mean falls in quantity, price and profits. In the long term, businesses might react to this by reducing supply (e.g. by closing some stores); this would cause a shift from S to S1. Prices might recover, but quantity would fall further.

Figure 6.5: The market for D-I-Y materials

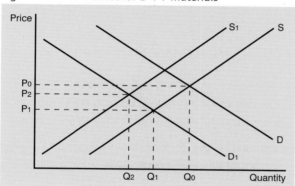

> The **profit signalling mechanism** is the way that potential profits (e.g. because existing firms have high profits) will attract entrepreneurs to a market and losses will lead businesses to consider leaving a market. This process shifts resource use between activities.

Our market model simplifies reality, making unrealistic assumptions, and we normally look at only one variable at a time. We rely on a '**ceteris paribus**' assumption which means that everything stays unchanged apart from the one thing we focus on. So, for example, when we look at supply in a market we assume that demand conditions stay fixed. It is quite possible, though, that both supply and demand conditions change at the same time. Although firms have some information about current demand, they can't always be confident about the shape of the demand curve and whether it is changing.

Such real world complexities should not cause alarm at this stage. The main focus is on the links between an initial change in a determinant of demand or supply and the resulting shift in one of the curves, in price and in quantity bought and sold. This will most often be concerned with the short term. Understanding what is going on and building confidence through repeatedly going through the sequence is the key. When you see that a price has changed, try to work out a mental image of the sequence involved.

> The simplifying **ceteris paribus** assumption freezes all variables other than the one being studied, avoiding complications from other changes.

Chapter 7

Price elasticity of demand (PED)

How price sensitive are games consoles?

Microsoft ran a promotion for the 2014 Christmas season in the United States, reducing the price of the Xbox console from $399 to $349. They have announced that the Xbox was the top selling console in December, with over a million sales.

At the start of January, the price reverted to $399. Surprisingly, a new promotion was announced two weeks later, with the price again reduced to $349. This time there is no set date for the promotion to end, though Microsoft stated clearly that this is a promotion rather than a permanent price cut.

Identify advantages of (i) a higher price and (ii) a lower price.

Suggest reasons why a promotion can have more impact than a price cut.

Elasticity is all about how much one variable changes in response to a change in another related variable.

We know that a change in price will bring about a change in quantity demanded. What we are looking at now is by *how much* the quantity demanded will change. This is what PED is all about.

We compare changes by looking at proportionate or percentage changes. This makes comparisons more meaningful. If we said that a small antiques shop and a large supermarket had both sold 10 more items in a day, this is probably very significant for the antiques shop but hardly noticeable for the supermarket as it will sell far more per day. Giving percentage changes is more meaningful.

We use a formula to work out PED.

Calculation of price elasticity of demand

$$PED = \frac{\text{\% change in quantity demanded}}{\text{\% change in price}}$$

Price elasticity of demand measures the responsiveness of quantity demanded to a change in price.

This will give a numerical answer which tells us the degree of price elasticity and we then refer to a good or a service as being price elastic or price inelastic.

If a chain of shoe shops reduces the price of a pair of shoes from £50 to £40 and sales per week increase from 100 pairs to 110 it is difficult to measure what has happened. But if we turn these changes into percentages we see that price has dropped by 20% and quantity has increased by 10%...

$$PED = \frac{\text{\% change in quantity demanded}}{\text{\% change in price}} \rightarrow \frac{10\%}{-20\%} = -0.5$$

In this example PED is price inelastic because the percentage change in quantity is less than the percentage change in price.

Numerical values of price elasticity of demand

Name	What happens	What it means	Numerical value
Price elastic	A price change causes a proportionately *bigger* change in quantity demanded	% change in Q is *greater* than the % change in P	Beyond -1
Unitary price elasticity	A price change causes the *same* proportional change in quantity demanded	% change in Q is the *same* as the % change in P	-1
Price Inelastic	A price change causes a proportionately *smaller* change in quantity demanded	% change in Q is *smaller* than the % change in P	Between 0 and -1

The answer in PED calculations is normally **negative**. This is because price and quantity move in opposite directions.

If price increases then quantity demanded will fall. If price decreases then quantity demanded will increase. Therefore one variable in the sum is always a minus, which makes the answer also a minus.

Illustration

A price elastic demand curve will look closer to horizontal, whereas a price inelastic curve is closer to vertical. As Figure 7.1 shows, cutting the price where demand is elastic causes a bigger rise in quantity demanded in relation to the change in price. With inelastic demand, prices increases cause smaller decreases in quantity demanded in relation to the price change.

Figure 7.1: Elastic and inelastic demand

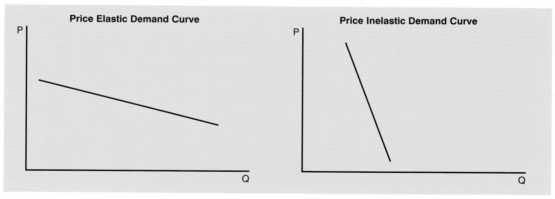

The factors influencing price elasticity of demand

Number and closeness of substitutes – The more substitutes a product or service has, the more price elastic it will be. The closeness of the substitute is important as well e.g. Nescafé and Maxwell House are quite close substitutes for instant coffees, but tea and coffee, which are both hot drinks, are not close substitutes for many people.

Luxury or necessity – Luxuries tend to be more price elastic and necessities tend to be more price inelastic. If the price of luxury goods such as a foreign holiday or a designer suit increases, you may be disappointed but you can probably do without. If the price of a necessity such as petrol increases, you may have little option but to keep buying it because you need to get to work.

Proportion of income spent on good – If a box of matches increases in price by 10% most people will either not notice or not be concerned; sales will hardly change. On the other hand if a new car goes up in price by 10% sales are likely to drop significantly and be price elastic.

Frequency of purchase – We tend to be more aware of the prices of things we buy frequently. Repeat purchases also increase the proportion of income spent on a product (see above). For these two reasons, things bought frequently tend to have higher price elasticity. It is no accident that milk is often discounted to attract shoppers, for example.

Time scale – In the short term many products and services will be more price inelastic than in the long term. Significant increases in the price of fuel leave consumers with little choice but to keep buying and so demand is price inelastic. Over time this higher price will lead to more economical vehicles and the development of alternative energy sources and the demand for fuel will become more price elastic.

Activity

A supermarket has bought too much Wensleydale cheese and even with yet another Wallace and Gromit advertising campaign, they have only shifted 50 packets in a day at £2.50 each. The next day they cut the price to £2.00 and sell 75 packets.

1. What is the PED for this particular cheese?

2. Was it a good idea to cut the price? Explain your answer.

3. Why might the PED for cheese be different from the PED for a pair of shoes?

The significance of price elasticity of demand for businesses

It is extremely important for a business to know what is likely to happen to its demand if it changes the price of its products or services. A business may have to change price for all sorts of reasons: changes in costs, actions of competitors and so on. It needs to know for planning purposes what may happen so that it can adapt its strategy.

Using PED data to predict what might happen to total revenue at different price levels will help with pricing decisions. Sometimes it will be possible to estimate PED using market research data. Otherwise, people in business have to work on a hunch. People with plenty of experience in the markets where they sell can be very good at deciding on a price without actually knowing the formula for PED. But they can also get a nasty surprise if their hunch turns out to be wrong.

Figure 7.2: Price cut where demand is elastic

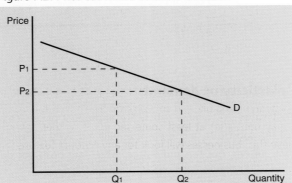

PED is likely to be more important to producers in mass markets where goods and services are likely to be standardised and have many substitutes, therefore price changes can have a much larger proportional effect on demand. Niche markets tend to rely much less on having a competitive price as they are by nature specialised and have fewer substitutes, therefore price changes have relatively little impact.

A business that can cut costs and reduce prices in a competitive market is going to do well. Demand is likely to be price elastic in such a market. Total revenue will rise significantly, as shown in Figure 7.2 when price is reduced from P1 to P2. The business can enlarge its market by attracting customers who previously bought substitutes. (Clearly in the reverse case, if it is not making a profit and tries to raise prices, it will make matters worse.)

A business with a very popular brand and great customer loyalty will be able to raise prices and increase total revenue. Demand is likely to be price inelastic in such a market. If it knows that this is the case, such a business will certainly not cut prices! With few close substitutes, it is effectively safe from competition and has a good deal of control over its price and quantity sold.

Businesses try to make demand for their products more price inelastic (less elastic). They do this by advertising and branding. They try to persuade their customers that there is no acceptable substitute. If they are successful they can increase the price without losing too many sales.

Figure 7.3: Price increase where demand is inelastic

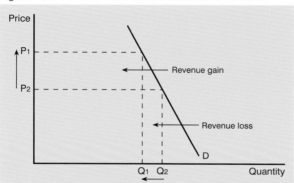

In a nearby supermarket, a 2 litre bottle of Coca-Cola sells at £1.95. Own brand cola is 45p and a value brand is 18p for 2 litres. Strong branding is a powerful asset.

In general, increasing price (if possible) is a good thing with price inelastic goods and services. More care is needed if demand is price elastic. The seller with inelastic demand can charge a higher price without losing sales to a significant extent. The opposite holds true... in general, decreasing price is bad for revenue and profit with price inelastic goods and services. Business selling products with price elastic demand will have less choice, and often less profit.

For individual businesses, high price elasticity goes together with being in a highly competitive market. Where there are many competing businesses, there will be plenty of good substitutes around. A price increase will be very likely to drive customers away. An obvious answer would be to cut costs and increase efficiency. This would be one way to maintain competitive advantage, though rivals are likely to be attempting the same approach.

From the consumers' point of view, competitive markets and price elastic demand force businesses to keep costs and prices down to the minimum possible and this is good for their standard of living. But you can see why someone in business may hope that at least some segments of their market will have relatively price inelastic demand. To achieve this, businesses will look for any product feature that will stand out and give customers the feeling of getting value for money. They will try to select a market position for their products where demand is as price-inelastic as possible.

The relationship between price elasticity of demand and total revenue

Changing price can dramatically affect total revenue, depending upon whether the demand is price elastic or price inelastic. A business needs to know what might happen and avoid making an expensive mistake.

Total revenue or TR is the amount of income generated by the sales of the business. It can be calculated by multiplying price (P) by quantity sold (Q). When P changes so too does TR. More importantly, the PED will determine whether the change is an increase or a decrease in TR.

Example

A business has a PED of -2. It is contemplating putting its price up from £10 to £11. Sales are currently 500 units per week.

Price goes up by £1 which is 10%.

Using our PED of -2 and the formula, we can work out that the change in Q will be -20%. (Another way to look at it is that -2 means the change in Q will be twice that of P.) So the actual fall in Q will be 100 units, to a new level of 400.

The TR **before** the price change is   £10 x 500 = £5,000

The TR **after** the price change is   £11 x 400 = £4,400

With a price elastic good such as this, a price rise reduces TR by £600, because the percentage fall in demand at the new price is higher than the percentage change in price.

Let's use the same example but this time the PED is 0.5

A 10% P rise will change sales by -5%, so the actual fall in Q will be 25 units to a new level of 475.

The TR **before** the price change is   £10 x 500 = £5,000

The TR **after** the price change is   £11 x 475 = £5,225

With a price inelastic good like this a price rise **increases** TR by £225.

If demand is **price elastic**	If demand is **price inelastic**
Increasing price would **reduce** TR	Increasing price would **increase** TR
Reducing price would **increase** TR	Reducing price would **reduce** TR

The government understands PED very well; that's why it puts indirect taxes on price inelastic goods such as alcohol, cigarettes and petrol and not price elastic ones! Taxes will increase the price of the goods and some consumers will decide to reduce the amount they buy. However, as the demand is price inelastic the fall in quantity demanded will be relatively small. In addition the total revenue and tax revenue for the government will increase.

The government puts indirect taxes on price inelastic goods such as alcohol.

Activity

Welsh Connections

Climbing DVDs are aimed at rock climbers, a small part of the overall outdoor leisure market. They are in many ways like snowboarding or BMX videos, only likely to be bought by committed enthusiasts with little or no crossover appeal to mainstream audiences.

This year's climbing films released on DVD range in price from £12.99 right up £19.99. This is somewhat unusual, as up until now, virtually all climbing DVD's regardless of length or quality, have been priced around the £20 mark. So why the change in pricing strategy?

Dave Brown is a leading maker of climbing films and has just released *Welsh Connections* at a price of £14.99. He said "The reason we priced Welsh Connections at £15 is because I've

slowly come to the view that £20 is simply too much to pay for a climbing film, even for the best ones. So selling our new film cheaper is something of a gamble. The hope is that more people will buy it. If £15 works this year then maybe we'll look at going even lower in the future, particularly if we move towards making the films only available to download."

1. What sort of market is the market for climbing DVDs? Explain your answer.

2. If Dave Brown is to be successful, what can you say about the P.E.D. for climbing DVDs?

3. If Dave Brown had sold 6,000 DVDs at £20 and sales increase to 9,000 units at the lower price of £15, what is the P.E.D. for the DVDs? What is the change in Total Revenue?

4. Does increasing his turnover *necessarily* mean that he will increase profitability? Explain your answer.

Chapter 8

Income elasticity of demand (YED)

Think!

What will you buy less of when you are better off? Why will you do this?

What might you only buy if you become seriously rich? How much do you want these things?

One of the factors affecting demand is a change in income. For most goods and services an increase in income increases quantity demanded. **Income elasticity of demand** is our measure of *how much* quantity demanded will change when income changes.

(In case you are wondering, Y is an accepted abbreviation for Income. I cannot be used for income as it is widely used to represent investment.) The formula used is similar to PED.

$$YED = \frac{\% \text{ change in quantity demanded}}{\% \text{ change in income}}$$

Income elasticity of demand measures the responsiveness of quantity demanded to a change in income.

This will give a numerical answer which tells us the degree of elasticity and we then refer to a good or a service as being income elastic or income inelastic…

Name	What happens	What it means	Numerical value
Income elastic	An income change causes a proportionately *bigger* change in quantity demanded	% change in QD is *greater* than the % change in Y	Greater than 1
Unitary income elasticity	An income change causes the *same* proportional change in quantity demanded	% change in QD is the *same* as the % change in Y	1
Income Inelastic	An income change causes a proportionately *smaller* change in quantity demanded	% change in QD is *smaller* than the % change in Y	Between 0 and 1

Unfortunately YED is a little more complex than PED. For most products and services quantity demanded rises as incomes rise and vice versa. These are called **normal goods**. They have a *positive* + YED value. Clothing is a normal good. There is good evidence that as incomes grow many people replace worn clothes sooner and add to their stock of clothing. If income falls, they buy fewer new clothes.

There are some products and services that do not behave like this – as incomes rise, quantity demanded falls and vice versa. These are called **inferior goods**. They have a *negative* – YED value.

Type of good	Incomes rise ↑	Incomes fall ↓
Normal	Quantity demanded ↑	Quantity demanded ↓
Inferior	Quantity demanded ↓	Quantity demanded ↑

An inferior good is not necessarily of poor quality but is seen as less attractive than some more expensive alternative. Public transport is often seen as an inferior good because if people's incomes fall they are more likely to sell their cars and switch to the bus. If their incomes rise again, they are likely to buy cars and stop using the bus. If people grow even richer, they might switch to a more luxurious car rather than a basic one.

What is seen as inferior is influenced by attitudes and incomes. Where income distribution is very uneven, a relative luxury to some groups can be an inferior good to others. Takeaway pizzas are a luxury to some, for example, whilst others see them as an inferior good compared to meals eaten out in restaurants.

Businesses selling inferior products and services tend to do well during a recession when incomes tend to fall and consumer confidence is low. Halfords saw an increase in sales during the recent recession as more motorists bought materials to do their own maintenance or a bike to commute and save money.

By contrast, businesses selling luxury income elastic goods such as exotic foreign holidays or designer clothes tend to do less well when there is an economic downturn. A rise in incomes as an economy recovers and grows tends to benefit businesses selling luxury products.

Factors that affect the degree of income elasticity

Whether the product or service is a luxury or a necessity is probably the main determinant of YED. Luxuries tend to be income elastic and to have high positive values for income elasticity. If real incomes rise, the demand for luxuries such as fast cars, expensive holidays abroad and high-tech electrical goods tends to rise at a proportionately greater rate. Many people who did not previously purchase these goods and services will now have enough money to do so.

Necessities are income inelastic and have a low positive value. If incomes fall then demand will only decrease slightly as many consumers will see little alternative other than to keep buying the necessity and cut down expenditure elsewhere.

Of course what constitutes a luxury or necessity varies between individuals and what was a luxury in the past may now be seen as a necessity. It is not that long ago that a mobile phone or satellite television were regarded as luxuries and the preserve of the well-off, many people today would see them as necessities.

Habits are slow to change. This helps to explain why many foodstuffs have low YED. The impact of increased income on demand for teabags is very low in the 21st century; a YED calculation would produce an extremely low figure. If we shift in time back to when teabags were first introduced, they were then a relative luxury. At that time, most people bought tea in packets of 'loose' leaves, which were cheaper per cup. Teabags would then have had a greater income elasticity of demand as extra income would have encouraged people to switch to them. Some people now see tea as an inferior substitute for coffee, but habitual tea drinkers are unlikely to switch.

Tea bags were a relative luxury.

As with price elasticity, the share of income spent on a good is again relevant. Teabags are relatively cheap and have low income elasticity. Housing is the biggest expense for most households. Real incomes fell for many households in the six years from 2008/9 onwards. The proportion of people living in houses they own or are buying has fallen in the same period. More people are forced to use rented homes as their incomes are insufficient to fund deposits and mortgage repayments. In this case there is a combination of PED (house prices have risen) and YED (incomes have fallen) at work.

As is often the case, confidence and expectations have an important impact on behaviour. A drop in income which is seen as a temporary blip will have little impact on consumer demand for most products. By contrast, a loss of confidence and the expectation that income might continue falling lead to bigger changes. As recession deepened in 2009, a gloomy mood led people to cut back on many relative luxuries. At the same time, demand for some items increased. For example, many workers bought thermos flasks and lunch boxes so they could save money by spending less on drinks and prepared food during the working day.

The significance of income elasticity of demand to businesses

Changes in individual incomes, for example from promotion or retirement, can be expected broadly to balance out across the community. Their impact on businesses will be slight. Where products have very low income elasticity, even more general changes in incomes will have little impact on demand and businesses.

Many businesses have at least some products with considerable income elasticity of demand, whether positive or negative. These will be affected by the long term trend to rising incomes and by shorter term recessions and booms. Awareness of income elasticities will help such businesses to anticipate demand and to plan strategies.

Value retail chain Poundland had a very good recession as customers felt secure in the belief that everything in the stores was a bargain. Turnover (sales) grew from £396m in 2007/8 to £997m in 2013/14, through a period when real incomes fell for typical households. Cheap often equates with inferior so rising incomes after recession might not be good news for Poundland. This led to experiments such as bringing in some higher price items, though the Advertising Standards Authority ruled in March 2015 that this made "Everything for £1" claims unacceptable. The company wants to maintain its current appeal but also do more to attract affluent customers.

The Greggs bakery chain found that its relatively inexpensive sandwiches, savouries, sausage rolls and pasties sold well in the recession, when expansion was rapid. From 2013, anticipating recovery, Greggs began transforming bakery stores into coffee shops, with an extended range of foods including healthier and more upmarket options. Greggs' profits continued to rise.

Anticipating that some customers would trade down to cheaper options during recession, some leading food producers agreed contracts to supply supermarket own label foods which would compete alongside their market leading brands. This allowed them to cater for consumers with both low and high income elasticity and to keep their production lines busy.

As incomes and standards of living rise in the long term, consumers expect more and better. Some long established products can become inferior, with consumers switching to improved alternatives.

The Youth Hostel Association (YHA) started in the 1930s, at a time when travel and holidays had a far smaller market. Young people were encouraged to visit and learn about the countryside. The original accommodation was in large single sex dormitories, visitors shared chores such as cleaning and arrival by car was frowned upon. As expectations have changed, the number of hostels has fallen from 300 to 200, there are now private rooms for families and couples, the chores have mainly gone and cars are welcome.

Spending on communications has more than doubled in the UK this century, but there is wide variation within this sector. A generation ago, fixed line telephone services and postage stamps were bought more frequently. The introduction of mobile phones, the internet and pay TV has transformed the communications market. Fixed line telephones now appear to be an inferior good, consumers spent 3bn minutes less talking on fixed line phones in the year to mid-2014 than the previous year.

BT (British Telecom), originally privatised with a monopoly of fixed line telephone services, has diversified into growing areas of the market. It has taken a leading role in the spread of fibre-optic internet connections, moved into pay TV and agreed to pay £12.5 billion for EE's mobile phone business. This enables BT to offer a bundle of communications services and also to expand the business whilst reducing its reliance on inferior goods.

In the long term, producers of inferior goods can decline, diversify or switch to products with positive income elasticity.

Activity

Consider BMW cars, use of YHA dormitory beds and fresh apples.

Income elasticity of demand for these 3 items is around -2, +0.1 and +1.7, but not in the same order. Match the 3 products with the most likely income elasticities, explaining your reasons.

Exam style question

OPEC

The Organisation of Petroleum Exporting Countries has 12 member countries, from wealthy Gulf States such as Saudi Arabia (its largest producer) to Nigeria and Venezuela. With production of up to half of global output and more than half of global oil exports, OPEC has had substantial market power in the early part of this century. US output fell for some years early in the century as existing wells became less productive. Oil dependent transport and electricity generating systems kept demand high. OPEC members found that restricting output and sales led to rising prices and profitability. Crude oil prices tripled between 2003 and 2008, rising above $120 per barrel.

Prices dipped during the recession from 2008, but recovered in 2011. Since then, the situation has changed. Fracking has increased US oil output and reduced their dependence on imports. Russia has expanded production and exports. Research and improvements in other energy sources have begun to increase the availability of substitutes for oil. This increases both price and income elasticity of demand. When oil prices dipped from the summer of 2014, OPEC members chose not to reduce output. Global supply exceeded demand and prices fell sharply through the winter.

Spring 2015 prices at around $50 per barrel were below production costs in difficult areas such as some UK North Sea oilfields. Half of US fracking production became unprofitable. Some analysts believe that leading OPEC producers hope to see higher cost competitors forced out of business; leading to reduced supply and rising prices. Others argue that OPEC has lost power. Smaller OPEC producers who depend on oil exports have little power to act without the Gulf States.

Questions

1. What is meant by 'market power'? *(2 marks)*
2. What is meant by income elasticity of demand? *(2 marks)*
3. Explain why oil prices tripled between 2003 and 2008 (paragraph 1). *(4 marks)*
4. Explain, using a diagram, why prices fell when global supply exceeded demand (paragraph 2) *(4 marks)*
5. Examine reasons why price elasticity of demand for oil is likely to increase in the long run. *(8 marks)*
6. Evaluate the impact of changing market conditions on North Sea oil output. *(10 marks)*

Chapter 9

Marketing: Product/service design

The Tata Nano

Basic early models minimised costs with: 2 cylinders, 1 wing mirror, no power steering, no radio, no airbags, no air-conditioning. The boot was only accessible through the interior and the fuel filler was under the bonnet. The introductory price of around £1,350 in India quickly rose close to £2,000.

Identify the priorities in the Nano's design mix.

Suggest reasons why sales have stayed below expectations, even in target markets such as India.

Marketing is a broad term that covers a wide range of business activities. The Chartered Institute of Marketing defines it as...

> "The management process responsible for identifying, anticipating and satisfying customer requirements profitably"

Do not confuse *marketing* with *sales* (exchanging output for money) or *advertising* (calling attention to a product or service). Marketing can include both of these but it has a much wider role and includes research, analysis, planning and the marketing mix.

Marketing has many purposes and they will vary from business to business. It is used to find out what customers want and then to design the goods and services that will best satisfy those wants and help to create a USP (Unique Selling Point). As well as coping with present consumer preferences it will also try to anticipate future changes and plan business strategy accordingly.

Marketing also focuses on maintaining and increasing sales and profits and maintaining a competitive advantage over other businesses. Marketing can try to create a strong brand that will justify a price increase (and reduce price elasticity of demand) and maintain and increase customer loyalty. Ultimately, marketing helps to ensure the survival and success of the business.

Figure 9.1: Marketing objectives

The marketing mix

> **The marketing mix** refers to all the elements of a firm's marketing strategy that are used to make their products more attractive to customers. They are often known as the **4Ps – Price, Product, Promotion** and **Place**.

We talk about the marketing *mix* because the ingredients will be used together in different combinations depending upon the needs and characteristics of a particular market.

The mix will be adapted in response to changes in the market such as changes in consumer behaviour and preferences, the actions of competitors, changing technologies and external economic influences such as the business cycle.

This first section of the marketing mix is about how businesses design and create desirable products that can be supplied to the customer. The umbrella word for all the processes involved is **operations management**. This includes:

The marketing mix.

- Design – making sure that the product is suited to market requirements, and adapting it when these change.

- Production – sourcing all the necessary inputs (either in-house or outsourcing from independent suppliers), creating a quality product and providing customer service.

Businesses want their product to have a competitive advantage and all aspects of the production process need to be cost-effective if competitive pricing is to be combined with profit. As new technologies become available businesses must be dynamic and adapt to become more efficient.

> **Operations management** covers all aspects of production including the sourcing of all inputs and the efficient organisation of all resources used in production.

Product or service design

Each individual product or service will be designed for a specific market or use. Product design involves working to a brief that sets out the priorities and criteria which will define the nature of the product.

These criteria are often described as the **design mix**, which combines three elements: function, aesthetics and economic manufacture.

Function – is the way in which the product performs. Products need to work, to be reliable and to do the job they were designed to do. If they do not they will not satisfy customers and may cease production.

Aesthetics – refers to the degree of beauty or style, as perceived by the user. Some products will consider this to be a key differentiating feature and will take precedence over the other two areas.

Economic manufacture – the product has to make a profit and must be capable of being manufactured at a cost below the selling price if it is to be viable.

> The **design mix** refers to the way in which function, aesthetics and economic manufacture are combined in the overall design.

Figure 9.2: Elements of the design mix

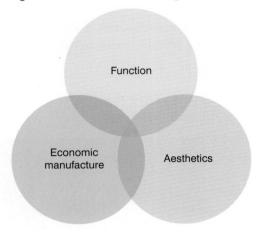

All products will contain the three elements of the design mix. However, the way in which the overall mix blends these elements depends partly on the aims of the designer and partly on the demands of the market segment it is produced for. For some products there will be much greater emphasis on, say, aesthetics than economic manufacture.

A pair of very fashionable shoes is selling almost entirely on its aesthetics; its function (keeping the feet dry and warm) may be a very minor consideration. If the shoes are exceptionally attractive, their aesthetic may sell them even if they are expensive to make. So they would be located in the clear green part of the aesthetic circle. By contrast, a pair of working boots needs first to be functional. Making them attractive could be a bonus for some buyers but others might prefer a no-nonsense functional look.

For many products all three elements in the design mix are important. You probably want your car to look good, perform well and be available at an affordable price. But for your toothpaste, probably only function and price matter.

The design mix applies to services as well as tangible products. Most retailers try to make their outlets pleasant and convenient to visit as well as offering attractive prices, though Aldi and Lidl have successfully given more emphasis to function. Hairdressers pay attention to their decor as well their hair styles and pricing, they work in an image conscious business.

Activity

Draw your own design mix diagram. Mark on the diagram with a cross where you think the following products would appear. Explain your decisions.

A Ferrari, Tesco's own brand Cola, Apple iPhone, a Big Mac, a diamond engagement ring, a bus.

Can you think of any products that would be placed exactly in the middle of your diagram?

Changes in the elements of the design mix to reflect social trends

Social trends refer to the way society as a whole behaves and the values that determine that behaviour. They are not static and are continually changing, sometimes slowly and sometimes quickly. They have an impact on the design mix and will alter the relative importance of the different elements.

Sustainability – As consumers have become more aware of environmental issues and the need to behave more responsibly, businesses have responded by adapting and changing their production. More emphasis is placed on sustainability and recyclability, energy saving has become paramount and its influence can be seen in everything from light bulbs to cars. Many consumers respond favourably to products which can claim to be environmentally friendly.

The Fairtrade movement has meant that many producers now think carefully about their choice of suppliers.

Alternative means of energy production have flourished with wind, solar, tidal and other green methods of energy generation proliferating. Buildings have better insulation; timber comes from sustainable reserves and many products now use recycled or upcycled materials. All of this has changed both the function and economic manufacture sectors of the design mix.

Plastic

When a 5p charge on plastic carrier bags was introduced in 2015 for large shops their use decreased significantly. In 2018, with public awareness of the environmental problems associated with plastic use and disposal, it is likely the charge will be extended to all shops.

There is also growing pressure over disposable coffee cups that have a plastic layer and all single-use plastic.

Should a similar charge be made for coffee cups? Should single use plastic be banned?

Ethical considerations – Consumer concern over the ways in which products are produced have influenced many producers to alter the supplies they use and the conditions under which they are made. The Fairtrade movement has meant that many producers now think carefully about their choice of suppliers. This has implications for economic manufacture. Simply finding the cheapest source of supply has become less acceptable. Businesses such as Nike and Primark have been attacked for using suppliers with exploitative wages and working conditions.

Rana Plaza

Bangladesh has many low cost garment factories. The eight storey Ran Plaza building in suburban Dacca was converted from shop and office use, with five garment factories moving in. The weight and vibration of machinery proved to be a problem. In April 2013 the building collapsed. The death toll rose to 1,129.

How much responsibility for this should western clothing brands that used these factories share?

How big is the danger of consumers turning against these brands?

The Ethical Trade Initiative (ETI) has many members including global companies with thousands of suppliers. Big businesses are keen to be seen to be acting ethically, motivated by a desire to act responsibly and/or concerns over brand image. Members sign up to follow ethical working practices and to ensure that workers in their supply chains are treated responsibly.

It is not just products but services that are changing as well, several banks make it their mission to create social and environmental benefits, by carefully choosing which companies and projects they provide finance to, examples include the Co-operative Bank and the Triodos Bank.

The rise in demand for organic foods, responsibly farmed meat and dairy produce, the number of vegetarians and the drive for healthier eating have all been driven by social trends and all have an impact on the design mix.

Economic – The financial crisis of 2008 and subsequent economic downturn have made economic manufacture more important for many market sectors. As consumers experience falling incomes and increased uncertainty over the future, price has become a more important element in the decision to buy or not. Cheap and functional has sometimes had more appeal than aesthetically pleasing alternatives at higher prices. As the Tata Nano example at the start of this chapter shows, it is possible to go too cheap and basically functional.

For businesses this has meant that costs need to be controlled and lowered, enabling prices to be cut. This can be seen in the rise of the cheaper supermarkets such as Lidl and Aldi and the way in which other supermarkets have responded by cutting prices and expanding their own budget ranges. Over a longer period the increasing price of fuel has led to more fuel efficient engines in cars as manufacturers responded to changing consumer preferences.

The International Monetary Fund counts 35 economies as developed, the other 150 for which data are recorded count as low or middle income countries. As a result, most of the world's population cannot afford to pay too much attention to the aesthetics of expensive items and looks mainly at functional and economic considerations. Thus, when Tata sought to spread car ownership wider in India it introduced the 'Nano' which was far cheaper than cars in developed countries but had fewer features and design flourishes. At the same time, people who are cash poor but time rich (where wages are very low) often have strong aesthetic traditions in their cultures.

Within cultures, the relatively rich often enjoy signalling their success and wealth by ostentatious consumption of items seen as supremely aesthetic and perhaps functional, but with very little regard to economic cost considerations. Thus the very small minority of Chinese billionaires have become leading global consumers of products such as Rolls Royce cars and expensive champagnes. It has been suggested that some buyers of the latest iPhone are doing so partly to make a statement about their own status.

Try this

People in different age groups generally have differences in their appearance – think of their use of clothing style, colour, hair and tattoos.

How much do you see this as due to changing attitudes at different stages in the lifecycle and how much do such differences reflect changing social trends?

Chapter 10

Branding and promotion

> ## Toilet roll tastes
>
> There are marked variations in the types of toilet roll bought in different countries. In many European countries consumers buy mainly own label and economy rolls. These take two thirds of sales in Germany, for example. British consumers prefer softness, luxury and branding. Andrex is the leading brand with more than a third of the market; Cushelle, Charmin and Velvet also sell well.
>
> Softer, thicker, premium brands use more trees and create more waste, but a temporary blip in their sales during the latest recession owed more to falling income levels than to environmental awareness. When leading supermarkets stock 'luxury' own label options made in the same factories as top brands, and presumably in the same way, sales are far lower than for top branded rivals.
>
> Why is branding so important for toilet rolls in the UK?
>
> Are German consumers being more sensible or just meaner?

Promotion is a key part of the marketing mix and has two purposes. It aims to inform customers and potential customers about the product and to persuade them to buy it. Often it is a combination of both. Promotion is all about raising customer awareness and increasing sales and profits for the business.

Branding is about creating an image of the product in the mind of the customer. The brand itself can be a name or an image but it should give the product an identity that is recognisable and positive. It should aid promotion and be an asset to the business in creating, maintaining and increasing sales.

Types of promotion

There are many different ways of promoting a product; the method chosen will depend on a number of factors. It will depend on whether the product is aimed at the mass market or a niche market, what size the business is and what budget it has available for promotion. It will also depend on the target market and the best way of reaching it.

Figure 10.1: Types of promotion

Advertising – There is a wide variety of advertising available to a business wanting to promote its products and services, ranging from the small and local to the huge and nationwide. Types of advertising include print, television, film, radio and billboards. Advertisements can be seen on vans, lorries and buses, they are in stations, motorway services, post offices and shops, in fact we are bombarded with promotional messages everywhere we go. Try counting the number you see on your way to or from school!

We are bombarded with promotional messages everywhere we go.

Advertising is likely to be seen by large numbers of people and is a quick way of reaching out to potential customers in a given area. It informs and persuades and is designed to increase sales. The advertising medium can be tailored to suit the needs and size of the market being targeted.

With so much advertising about, it can be difficult for an advert to get noticed. It can be hard to know just how effective your advertising is or how many people have seen it, and some advertising is very expensive. Now that it is no longer necessary to watch television 'live', many people will fast-forward through the adverts, and newsagents and supermarkets provide bins where you can tip the unread advertising leaflets before buying magazines and papers.

Sales Offers – These are usually short-term techniques, often in the form of incentives, to encourage customers to buy. They can include money-off coupons; buy one get one free offers (BOGOF), discounts, free samples and special offers.

These all lower the price temporarily, if genuine. The idea is to tempt customers to buy now and save money; the business hopes that the cheaper goods will lead to rival products being ignored and that after the offer some customers will have developed loyalty and will continue to buy.

The main drawback to this form of promotion is that some consumers will simply take advantage of the cheaper prices and stock up, then wait for the next special offer. This is likely to reduce profitability and may cancel out any advantages gained.

Digital – The profusion of digital media has meant that a whole new raft of promotional activities is available to a business. Digital promotion is aimed at users of the internet, mobile phones or other digital devices such as tablets and game systems. Methods include Facebook pages run by the business itself; online advertising, 'advergaming' (a video game which in some way contains an advertisement for a product), social media and viral marketing.

The main advantage of digital promotion is that it is cheap and has the potential to reach large numbers of people. The internet never sleeps and reaches potential customers at all times and all over the world. Once started, a digital campaign can take on a life of its own and spread from peer to peer without any further effort from the originator.

There is a lot of competition on the internet and some analysts think that it may not be that effective. At the end of 2014 Google published their research which showed that 56.1% of the adverts it showed were not looked at by anybody, either being scrolled past immediately or not even reaching the screen. Google claimed to run about 30 billion ads per day! Some people still distrust content from the internet.

Sponsorship – Businesses gain publicity by financially supporting an event, activity or person. The business name gets advertised along with the event and generates a positive brand image. This is common for sporting events and becoming more popular with the arts and television.

The advantages of sponsorship are that it reaches a wide range of people, for the big sporting events this means millions of people are seeing your name. It can also bring positive connotations that will enhance your image and reputation. The YouTube clip of Felix Baumgartner's record balloon jump has been seen over 38 million times giving the sponsor Red Bull, massive publicity.

The downside is that sponsorship can be very expensive compared to other forms of promotion and there is no guarantee that consumers will rush out and buy your product because they see the name on an event programme. Sponsorship can also backfire; Nike sponsored Tiger Woods the golfer but dropped him when revelations about his private life risked damaging the brand.

> **Think!**
> Which are the first examples of sponsorships that come to your mind?
> Do you use the brands that are promoted in this way?

Direct sales – This involves direct contact between a sales person and the potential customer. It can involve door to door but is normally done over the phone. To be successful a good list of 'leads' is needed to avoid wasting time.

The main advantage of direct selling is that the message can be adapted to suit the consumer as the conversation progresses. The salesperson can answer individual queries and tailor their sales approach to maximise the chances of success.

Many people dislike direct sales and the 'high-pressure' sales pitch of some callers. There is currently a great deal of ill feeling to cold callers and further regulation may curb this method of promotion. It is also relatively expensive, involving large sales teams.

Public relations (PR)

Public relations involve liaising with the press and media and providing information about the company. Many businesses have PR departments or use an outside agency to promote their products or services by getting the media to mention them in a positive light without payment. News stories about the business are then read or seen by many people. Publicity may be given to fund raising events, good works or initiatives that keep the name of the business in the public eye.

It can be a cheap method of promotion, even though the PR department or company will cost money. By comparison with the cost of advertising it is very cost effective. When Apple launch a new product they have little need to promote it as the world's media pick up the story and do the job for them.

A problem with PR is that it cannot be as precisely targeted as other forms of promotion. The decline in print media means that there is no guarantee that a story or feature will be seen by potential customers. It is not always possible to control what is said and businesses that rely on the media for good publicity may find themselves trying to control the spread of negative press stories as well.

Types of branding

There are a number of different types of branding that can be identified although some brands could fit a number of categories.

- **Product branding** – Product brands can be very specific and refer predominantly to a single product recognised by that name. Examples include Coca-Cola, Marmite and Manchester United.

- **Multiple branding** – This is when a business uses a range of brand names for its products. Many consumers are unaware that different brands are all owned by the same company. Unilever has over 400 brands including Dove, Flora, Surf and Knorr. Mendelez has Cadbury, Oreo, Trident and Milka.

- **Umbrella branding** – An umbrella brand is one that uses the same brand name for a range of different but related products. Sometimes referred to as family branding, examples include Dove toiletries, Nescafé and Virgin.

- **Corporate branding** – The name of the business is the brand and allows new products to be recognised and accepted by consumers who already know and trust the brand such as Mercedes, Apple and Sony.

- **Own label branding** – This is common amongst supermarkets with brands such as Tesco's finest, Sainsbury's basics and Sainsbury's Organic SO.

- **Personal branding** – Sometimes individuals become so well-known and identifiable they become their own brand. David Beckham or if you prefer, 'brand Beckham', has been applied to clothing, fragrances and whisky amongst other things.

The benefits of strong branding

Added value

> **Added value** is the difference between the selling price of a product or service and the costs of its material inputs.

Strong brands are valuable assets: they create wealth for their companies, communities and economies. A strong brand adds value by enabling a higher price to be charged. Profitability is increased. It creates a difference between the brand and its rivals, creating a competitive advantage. This makes it less vulnerable to competition and forges a stronger bond with its customers.

Ability to charge premium prices

It is no coincidence that leading brands are usually more expensive than rival products. Heinz baked beans, Coca-Cola and Apple all charge premium prices. They all have substitutes that cost less but consumers are reluctant to accept them in place of the strong brand to which they have loyalty. They are happy to pay the higher price. For some brands and consumers the higher price is a reflection of the brand's desirability and the customer's social standing in being able to afford it.

Reduced price elasticity of demand

The main determinant of Price Elasticity of Demand (PED) is the number and closeness of substitutes. The more there are available the higher the PED. Strong branding persuades the consumer that any substitute products are less acceptable and therefore the PED will be reduced, making demand for the brand less price elastic.

Figure 10.2: Successful branding

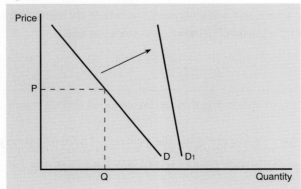

Ways to build a brand

Unique selling points (USPs)/differentiation

> A **Unique Selling Point** (**USP**) is any feature of a product or service that sets it apart from its competitors.

It may seem obvious but a USP has to be unique, it is not shared with rival products or services and is strong enough to keep existing customers satisfied and be able to attract new ones. The USP is closely connected with the positioning of the brand (how it is perceived by consumers in relation to rival brands). A USP can re-position the brand and leave a clear gap from the competition.

Apple is one of the best examples of branding in the world and in 2015 the most valuable brand. Yet it has not always been the first to develop new technology. Its great success is developing the brand. This brand is built on a range of attractive, simple yet functional products with a distinctive logo. Apple's shops are also different, with simple displays, lots of bright lighting, and little colour except for white and grey. They reinforce Apple's USP: sleek, stylish and functional.

Advertising

Advertising reinforces the brand image in people's minds. Clever advertising creates images and feelings that reinforce the positive aspects of the brand, increasing its desirability and value. TV advertising is especially good at this; it is no coincidence that many famous film directors made commercials in their early years. Ridley Scott made the first Apple commercial way back in 1984!

Sponsorship

By sponsoring sporting and cultural events or individuals, businesses gain a lot of useful exposure to the public. The brand name is constantly repeated in connection with the event and is more likely to be remembered by the potential customer. Red Bull sponsor a range of extreme sports including cliff diving, BMX, skiing, flying, mountain biking and skateboarding. They also sponsor one off events such as the Erzberg Enduro off-road motorcycle race where less than two percent of entrants finish the course. All of this helps to create a strong brand image that is seen as cutting edge, skilful, daring and cool, appealing to their main target market of young adult males.

Changes in branding and promotion to reflect social trends

Viral marketing

Viral marketing describes any strategy that encourages individuals to pass on a marketing message to someone else. This creates the potential for rapid and exponential growth in the spreading of the promotional message. Named after the way real viruses multiply rapidly, the message can quickly reach millions. It has also coined the phrase 'going viral' which means that something has suddenly taken off and is being seen and talked about by many individuals.

Methods of viral marketing include video clips, emails, texts, web pages and interactive games. Some viral marketing campaigns have been phenomenally successful. The video clip 'Evian baby and me' has so far been watched over 102 million times on YouTube.

The use of social media

It is of course possible to advertise on social media but the main way of building a strong brand is to create an online following that will respond and pass on brand information. Successful brands are the ones that create a community around their brand, after all this is the purpose of a social network. They post the latest news along with special offers, giveaways, coupons, games; and give participants an opportunity to interact with each other and leave opinions and views. The important point is that this is not traditional advertising but it does reinforce the brand.

In many ways social media has changed the way society works; it has also transformed some areas of business practice as well. A survey in 2014 claimed that 97% of businesses used social media for marketing purposes with Facebook and LinkedIn being the most popular vehicles. More than half of marketers who've been using social media for at least 3 years report it has helped them improve sales. Business expenditure on social media is expected to reach $5 billion in 2015.

Emotional branding

Emotional branding is the term given to the creation of brands that appeal to a consumer's emotional nature rather than their logical side. The consumer may not be able to articulate why they feel such brand loyalty in rational terms but there is a strong attachment there, emotional branding affects people at a hidden level. Needs such as love, power, happiness and ego gratification are part of our subconscious nature, we seek to fulfil those needs and marketers create brands that appeal to those needs.

The use of music and image can create a powerful and impressionistic image that appeals to the heart. Factual content or information may well be secondary to the creation of a positive feeling. One of the most successful emotional branding campaigns is MasterCard's 'Priceless' series which has been running very effectively for 17 years.

As Dale Carnegie said: *"When dealing with people, let us remember we are not dealing with creatures of logic. We are dealing with creatures of emotion."*

Coca-Cola mini cans

Coca-Cola recently launched a range of its drinks in mini-cans aimed at those customers counting calories and becoming more health conscious. The mini-can isn't dearer than the regular sized can but is more expensive per ml of drink. Coke had done its research and found that the mini-cans reduced the amount of guilt that a consumer felt for snacking, while minimising the chances of overeating. The company understood the needs of its customers and provided a solution.

Peroni

When South African drinks giant SABMiller bought a little-known Italian brewery, Peroni, a marketing consultancy was given the job of building the brand up. They identified the values and qualities that consumers liked about Italy. The result was a series of campaigns that focused on Italy's associations with style, fashion, beauty and 'dolce vita' coolness. As a result Peroni is now a well-known brand and selling well in 20 global markets.

L'Oréal

L'Oréal is increasing sustainable resource use at each stage of production. This involves ethical policies and the selection of new ingredients from sustainable sources. It is seeking a 50% reduction in greenhouse gas emission, waste and water consumption per finished product. The company has a fair trade policy and a commitment to local communities.

1. Explain how Coca-Cola mini-cans, Peroni and L'Oréal have added value to their brands.

2. What is likely to have happened to the price and PED of these products?

3. Can you see any drawbacks to this?

4. To what extent are these businesses using emotional branding?

Chapter 11

Pricing strategies

Prices

The Apple Watch was launched with prices starting at £299 and rising to £13, 500 for the solid gold version.

Three local petrol stations are all currently selling their brand of petrol for 113.5p a litre.

Ufit protein shake drinks are currently being sold at an introductory price of £1 rather than the usual price of £2.

The price of a new Triumph Tiger Sport motorcycle is £9,995

The school's Young enterprise company has just calculated that it needs to sell its hand-made bracelets for £5.

What factors do you think have influenced the prices of the products and services above?

For many consumers price is an important factor when deciding which product to choose. It may be that finding the cheapest option is important. Alternatively, a high price may denote exclusivity and desirability. The pricing strategy is almost always an important aspect of marketing. The ability to set price can be a valuable source of competitive advantage.

> A **pricing strategy** is the approach which a business decides on for setting the price of its product or service.

Types of pricing strategy

Cost plus (calculating mark-up on unit cost)

To an extent all businesses are influenced by their costs when it comes to price. In the long term price needs to be above costs to generate the profit needed for survival. Cost plus pricing is based on how much percentage profit the business decides to target. This is then added to the costs of the product e.g. a business wanting to make 20% profit with an average cost of £10 per unit would set the price at £12. The 20% is often referred to as the mark-up.

This method is easy and simple and ensures that each unit sold yields a profit over the calculated cost. There are, however, drawbacks to this strategy. Simply picking a mark-up could be disastrous if it does not take into account the market or the prices of competitors. It does not guarantee that all products will be sold; if they are not, then a loss may be made. Mark-ups also vary widely between industries and firms.

> Restaurants commonly mark-up the price of wine by three or more times its cost to them. When tennis player Andy Murray opened a smart hotel, the mark-up on some wine was 6 times the cost.
>
> Why are restaurants and hotels able to add a big mark-up to the price of wine?
>
> What would happen to a greengrocer who added a 600% mark-up to the cost of fruit?

Price skimming

Skimming the market means charging a very high initial price for the product. The idea is to get as much profit as possible while the product or service is relatively unique in the market. This only works for products that consumers see as new and different. Demand will be high and some people will be willing to pay a high price to acquire the unique product. Such people are referred to as 'early adopters'.

Price skimming is only possible for a limited period, rival businesses will develop their own versions of the product and as more competitors enter the market the price will normally fall. This type of strategy is commonly found in the consumer electronics and pharmaceutical markets and is more likely to work for a well-established, well-known business with an innovative product. Some businesses keep skimming by frequently 'improving' their products with new and 'better' versions.

Penetration

Penetration pricing is used by businesses which want to enter a market where similar products already exist. The new entrant sets a lower price than the competition to entice consumers to give their product a try, rather than buy their previous brand. This is intended to build market share and get the brand known.

Once established, the new entrant will probably raise their price to a more profitable level. If consumers have grown to like the brand they may well continue to buy the product when the price rises. How much the price can be increased depends on the strength of brand loyalty and the reaction of competitors.

Predatory

Sometimes called destroyer pricing, this is a tactic used by a dominant business either to eliminate a competitor or to prevent a rival from taking market share. It involves setting very low prices, perhaps even below the costs of production, for as long as it takes to 'destroy' the competition. Once the competitor leaves the market, prices can be increased again.

This relies on the dominant business being able to sustain the pain of very low prices for longer than its rival; which is possible when a business can cross-subsidise from other activities. For example, a successful TV subscription service could cross-subsidise a newspaper owned by the same group of companies. Predatory pricing is illegal under competition law. However, proving that behaviour is predatory is difficult. The accused firm may simply claim that they are being very competitive.

Competitive

For a business facing strong competition from similar products, the pricing options available are likely to be limited. The prices charged by its competitors have a strong influence on what can be done. Competitive pricing means looking at the prices that the competition is charging and making your prices similar to theirs. For example, 'price matching' promises by businesses such as supermarkets and John Lewis stores are common in competitive markets.

Any attempt to raise prices above the competitive level, when products are seen as close substitutes, can result in a fall in sales as customers move to now cheaper substitutes. To improve profitability in this situation, a business can either focus on cutting costs by operating efficiently or find some means of differentiation to make its products or services more attractive than rivals.

Psychological

Psychological pricing uses a price signal to persuade customers to buy the product. It is commonly used to make the price seem better value than it actually is by rounding it down slightly. Instead of charging £10 for a book the price is £9.99, a car may be £14,995 rather than £15,000. Prices ending in 9, 95, 97, 99 are sometimes called 'charm prices'. Setting a price a couple of pence below an evenly numbered price such as £10 is reported to increase sales by up to 30%. A survey in The Marketing Bulletin found that 60% of prices ended in the digit 9, 30% ended in the digit 5, 7% ended in the digit 0 and the other seven digits together accounted for only a little over 3% of prices used.

A variation on this is to combine an eye-catchingly low 'headline' price with extra charges that increase revenue and profits. One example is budget airlines selling cheap tickets then charging heavily for luggage, choice of seats or on-board snacks. Others include restaurant wine or metallic paint on cars. Psychological pricing is useful when customers are looking for value for money. By contrast, some high-end products avoid being seen as cheap if they feel that a high price can reinforce customers' expectations of high quality.

Many budget airlines offer low 'headline' prices but then add extra charges for items such as luggage, choice of seats and onboard snacks.

Pricing strategy summary

Competitive pricing	Accepting the market price or following a price leader where products are very similar.
Cost-plus	Calculate average cost per unit and then add a profit margin. Not quite as simple as it sounds.
Penetration	Setting a low price with limited short term profit in order to build market share before switching to a more profitable price.
Predatory	Very low prices, often below cost, intended to drive competitor(s) out of business. Illegal in the UK but hard to prove the intent.
Psychological	Setting a price designed to put notions of value (or exclusiveness) into the minds of consumers.
Skimming	A high price, perhaps temporarily, aimed at getting extra revenue with limited sales.

Think!

Which of these strategies could entail deliberately setting prices below costs?

How can businesses sometimes have no option but to sell at a loss?

Factors that determine the most appropriate pricing strategy for a particular situation

The strategy chosen will depend on a range of factors, centring on the nature of the product or service and the market. The amount of competition the business faces will be important. Less competition and fewer close substitutes mean that a business will have more control over price.

More competition and more substitutes reduce the ability of the business to set its own price, it will be more influenced by what its rivals are doing. The product or service itself can be crucial. If it has a competitive advantage via differentiation, a USP or a strong brand, control over price is greater. Finally, external factors such as the state of the economy or government policies can affect consumers and the prices they will pay.

With a long established product, the pricing decision will be affected by its position in the market. If it is a market leader, it may be possible to charge a relatively high price and rely on brand loyalty to maintain sales. But with a new and unknown product, the price has to be competitive in order to establish a presence in the market.

Number of USPs/amount of differentiation

Nearly all businesses try in one way or another to make their product different to the competition. Once that is achieved, customers will base their buying decisions on factors other than price alone. The extent to which people will pay more is affected by the strength and quality of the differentiation. For many consumers there may not be much to choose from between washing powders and the choice of which to buy may be influenced by the price more than the brand. Those who believe that one brand washes cleaner or leaves clothes softer will pay extra for their brand.

When the Dyson vacuum cleaner appeared on the market it was much more expensive than most of its rivals, yet it sold well and has become a leading brand. What made customers buy it was its combination of USPs and product differentiation, it didn't need a bag and didn't lose suction power as it got full. Not only that, it looked completely different with brightly coloured plastics and futuristic looks.

Price elasticity of demand

PED is important to any business contemplating its pricing strategy. A business facing price elastic demand will be wary of raising prices as that will cause a more than proportional fall in demand and a fall in total revenue. At the same time, there may be a temptation to cut price to gain a more than proportional increase in sales and a rise in total revenue. In this case care must be taken not to reduce profitability as extra sales will also mean extra costs.

 WATCH OUT!

Always remember that extra revenue does not guarantee extra profits if costs rise as well.

For businesses with price inelastic demand there is more scope for a higher price. Apple, for example, has the ability to keep skimming with high prices long after similar products have entered the market. Frequently changing and 'improving' products reinforces differentiation and price inelasticity of demand. The first iPhones reached the market in 2007, by September 2014 the iPhone 6 was available and some additional changes had been made between major launches.

Level of competition in the business environment

Directly linked to PED is the level of competition. Lots of competition necessitates a competitive pricing strategy for fear of losing sales to rivals with similar products. This is why a USP or a strong brand is important. Apple has many substitutes but some consumers are reluctant to buy them because of brand loyalty. A business with little competition has a degree of monopoly power and has much more freedom with its pricing strategy.

Strength of brand

There is a strong correlation between the strength of a brand and the ability of a business to set a premium price. In previous chapters the importance of the brand as a means of promotion was considered. Promotion and the development of a strong brand can enable businesses to set prices above competitors without damaging sales. This is because substitutes become less acceptable and so demand becomes less price elastic. This is why products such as Heinz baked beans; Coca-Cola and Dulux paint can charge premium prices despite the presence of many cheaper substitutes.

The stage a product has reached in its life cycle will also influence pricing and profitability. This is considered in Chapter 13.

Costs and the need to make a profit

Profits are the reward for business success and also provide a source of funding for future development. If, for example, owners of a struggling business feel that it could benefit from expensive promotion activities, a lack of profit could block financing extra promotion internally. Banks and other lenders look for profitability to have confidence that any loan will be repaid, so external finance might be difficult too.

New businesses frequently need time to become established and to reach profitability. Failure to ensure sufficient finance to fund unprofitable early years commonly leads to rapid failure. Established businesses will often find that changing conditions bring upward pressure on their costs or downward pressure on their revenue. Failure to respond is likely to turn profit to loss, leading eventually to inability to meet costs and so to bankruptcy.

Cutting costs is possible, for example by using cheaper materials, by closing branches, by reducing research and development or by cutting marketing expenditure. The danger here is that each of these cuts can bring additional problems. If the quality of the product falls, its availability is reduced, it is left behind by competitor innovation or its image becomes weaker, revenue is also likely to fall.

> **Think!**
> How could each of these changes damage a struggling restaurant chain?

A desperate business will sometimes slash prices as a short term means of survival. This can help to get immediate debts settled. However, long term success and survival depends on a marketing mix which includes a pricing strategy to keep revenue ahead of costs.

Changes in pricing to reflect social trends

Online sales

The spread of the internet and computer technology imposed far reaching changes on pricing strategies and prices in general. For the first time, consumers had access to a much wider range of goods than previously, and could compare a full range of prices and availability. Online sales have broadened choice and competition, often making markets more price competitive. Traditional shops can no longer charge higher prices just because they are the only local supplier. Consumers can see what the going rate is and businesses have to have a real reason for charging any more than this.

The other side of this gain for consumers is that businesses can also benefit from computer technology and the internet. The amount of information they can gather on customers is one source of power. Firms can learn our spending habits and much more about us. In 2012 an outraged father (near Minneapolis, USA) formally complained to a store manager about his High School student daughter being sent advertisements for baby products. A few days later he withdrew the complaint when the daughter confirmed that she was pregnant.

Software also gives online businesses ways to vary prices between customers, based on what they are likely to be willing to pay. This reinforces the trend in markets such as travel and recreation for prices to be based on the consumer as well as the product.

Price comparison sites

One development of online sales has been the creation of price comparison sites. These give even more power to the consumer by enabling them to see a range of prices at a glance. Many businesses have deliberately obscured the position by using complex pricing structures that make accurate comparisons difficult. In 2014 the energy regulator Ofgem forced energy companies to simplify their bills. Even price comparison websites have come under fire as they have been accused of hiding the best energy deals from consumers because they earn more commission from other suppliers. Nevertheless it is true that these sites and the internet have driven prices down overall.

New products

The following new products were developed using crowdfunding.

For each product suggest the most appropriate pricing strategy, explaining your choice and pointing out any potential disadvantages.

Seedsheet offers gardeners a simple 'plug and plant' approach. The service enables customers to enter the location of their garden (to identify which plants will thrive), and plan their bed using the online garden-building software. A custom Seedsheet is then made to match the customer's requirements, which when delivered is just unrolled onto the soil and watered.

Announced in September 2014, US-based **Palate Home's Smart Grill** is designed to ensure that food is cooked to perfection. The sensor-equipped device connects to an app, through which the user programmes what's being cooked and their cooking preference. The grill can sear meat, and automatically hold food for up to an hour once cooked.

Developed in the US **HEXO+** is a camera carrying drone that follows and films its users. Once people have entered the way they wish to be filmed, the drone follows their every move, automatically maintaining the desired framing.

Distribution

Distribution is one of the key elements of the marketing mix (sometime known as 'Place') and is all about getting the product to the right place at the right time. It might seem rather mundane compared to other elements of Price, Promotion and Product but in some ways it is more important. If, for example, the local supermarket runs out of milk or bread, customers feel let down and both the shop and its suppliers lose potential business.

If the customer can't access an item to buy it, or if stocks run out halfway through a campaign, it doesn't matter how good your product is, how keenly priced or how well promoted. Distribution is increasingly complex as globalisation shrinks the world and goods and services often have long journeys. Consumers are used to having products available on demand. For today's businesses distribution is crucial.

> **Distribution** is concerned with getting products to the right place for consumers and at the right time.

Distribution channels

> A **distribution channel** is the route taken by the product as it moves from the producer to the customer.

Figure 12.1: The Four-Stage distribution channel

Wholesalers buy in large quantities from different producers and have the facilities to keep a large range of stock. They then break this down into smaller bundles for delivery to retailers who then sell on to the customer. This traditional method is often used for confectionery and groceries, for example.

The big advantage of using a wholesaler is that the producer can concentrate on production and does not have to worry about dealing with many different retailers. It also saves on storage and warehousing costs for the producer. Wholesalers know their retailers and can provide useful market information back to the producer. The main drawback from the producer's viewpoint is that the wholesaler effectively markets the product and this may not always be as effective as the business would like, and of course, the wholesaler reduces the profit margin as they take their share.

Figure 12.2: The Three-Stage distribution channel

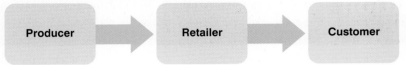

In this model there is no wholesaler, the producer sells directly to the retailer who then sells to the customer. This is found in many modern markets and there are two main variations dependent on where the retailer buys from. In the case of a product such as cars there is one producer, for example Skoda, who supply Skoda dealerships. This method enables the producer to directly control the supply and marketing of their products via limited and regulated outlets. Whilst this may be good for the producer it does restrict competition and choice for the consumer. In the past this has led to investigation by the competition authorities.

The alternative approach has supermarket chains, Amazon and others buying from many different producers. In this case the power in the market lies with the very large retailers who can drive down costs with their huge buying power. This can then be passed on to the consumer in the form of low prices, wide choice and convenience. However, many have criticised businesses such as Amazon and Tesco, claiming that they lead to the closure of traditional retail outlets.

Figure 12.3: The Two-Stage distribution channel

Traditionally such a distribution channel involved businesses such as a local baker or butcher selling directly to the customer. Farm shops and factory outlets are other ways of producers selling directly to customers. Producers have to do more, spreading beyond just making their product, but they benefit from maximising the revenue they keep by not having to share with wholesalers or retailers. Customers may gain from cheaper goods and fresher produce.

This distribution system has gained in popularity with the growth of the internet (see next section).

Changes in distribution to reflect social trends

Online distribution

Figure 12.4: Advantages of online distribution

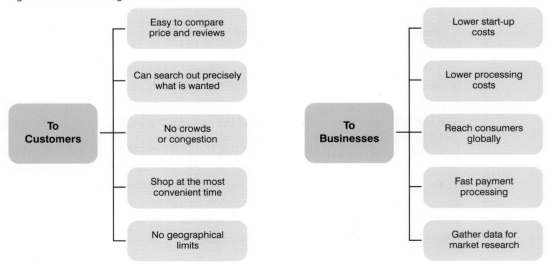

In 2014, 38 million UK adults accessed the internet each day. This was 76% of the adult population and was double the number from 7 years earlier. Many of those 38 million people sometimes shop online. Online spending has grown close to £50bn p.a. and is increasing at 15% p.a. This represents a major shift in the pattern of spending and distribution. Systems have now evolved to supplement home delivery – which necessitated having someone there to receive items – with convenient collection points. Search engines can find just about anything at the click of a mouse, offering convenience and often good value. Consumers without internet access are now at a disadvantage.

Businesses that use eRetailing have the option to cut out middlemen and their share of revenue, or to use established online platforms such as eBay and Amazon. Start-ups can be faster and cheaper with no need for retail premises. Order processing can be simple, regardless of the distance from consumers. Valuable data on consumer choices and spending can easily be collected. Many established retailers have seen the value of online presence and many now combine 'bricks and clicks' – traditional stores alongside an eRetailing option.

> **eRetailing** is an umbrella term for all forms of online sales to consumers.

We now have 'dark stores', distribution centres that cater exclusively for online shopping. They may actually be very well lit, but they don't need pleasant layouts to attract customers and their working conditions have often been criticised. A dark store, usually a large warehouse, is not open to the public and can operate 24 hours a day. Orders are received online and teams of pickers collect the products for delivery by courier or mail.

Amazon's largest dark store, in Baltimore (USA) has a total area of over 1 million square feet. Tesco was the first to open a UK grocery dark store in 2006, and now has 47.5% of the growing online grocery market. This will change as other major supermarkets are opening more dark stores and are catching up.

Changing from product to service

The distribution systems outlined above are mainly concerned with getting physical products from the maker to the final consumer. The long term UK trend has been for manufactured products to form a declining share of total output. Services now make up 80% of all production. Major service categories include creative services, education, health, social services, financial services, hotels and restaurants, tourism and transport.

Some service sectors mirror the recent changes in physical goods distribution. Whereas people once visited their bank branch fairly regularly, online banking now has a significant market share. Credit and debit cards have reduced the role of cash, but more than 66,000 'Link' cash machines (ATMs) are available for consumers who wish to physically withdraw cash from accounts. Downloads of music and films have reduced the reliance on CDs, DVDs and visits to the cinema.

Downloads of music have reduced the reliance on CDs.

For many of us, a visit to the cinema is still an attractive use of recreation time and multiplexes have evolved to improve the experience they offer. Personal services such as hairdressing, dental treatment and tattoos require a physical meeting with the provider. Most people still prefer a personal consultation with a doctor to the systems of remote access which are now available. Tastes may change for future generations.

Distribution is itself a service, getting products to consumers at a suitable time and place in an appealing and convenient way. As technology and tastes change, so too must distribution if it is to function effectively. The number of empty shops in High Streets and the changing use of many premises (e.g. more take-away food outlets and less public houses) is evidence of some of the changes taking place.

Adding more channels

Starbucks, the now famous coffee chain, started with only one distribution channel. The stores were owned, staffed and run directly by the company and operated profitably. Later Starbucks opened another distribution channel by franchising operations to other venues: airports, bookstores, and college campuses. The company recently signed a licensing agreement with Albertson's food chain to open coffee bars in its supermarkets.

Staying with one channel

The alternative is to stick to one channel and develop it with very tight controls. The Rolex Watch Company could easily place its famous watches in many more outlets. Instead it restricts its coverage to only high-end jewellers who are separated geographically and who agree to carry a certain level of inventory (= stocks), use certain display patterns, and place specific levels of local advertising.

Discuss the possible advantages and disadvantages to both Starbucks and Rolex of their distribution channels.

Chapter 13

Marketing strategy

Marketing objectives are the longer term marketing goals and targets that a business is trying to reach. Marketing strategies are used to meet the marketing objectives set by the business. If the objective is to increase sales then the marketing strategy used to achieve this might be a promotional campaign aimed at its target customers.

The Product Life Cycle

The human life cycle is something that we all go through; we are conceived, born into the world and then we grow and gradually mature. As we move through maturity we reach the peak of our powers and then as we age we begin to decline and eventually we cease to exist. The product life cycle follows much the same path. Somewhere an engineer, inventor or entrepreneur conceives an idea for a product or service, it needs to be developed and tested before being launched onto the market where hopefully it begins to grow and mature. A mature product generates strong sales but it will eventually decline as better and more efficient substitutes emerge. Ultimately it will exit the market. Sometimes the product life cycle is short when the product is rapidly overtaken by technology and innovation such as a mobile phone. By contrast some products last for decades, the Mars bar is still going strong over 80 years later!

The **Product Life Cycle** shows the different stages a product passes through as it moves from an idea to the end of its life. There are five stages associated with it: Development, Introduction, Growth, Maturity and Decline. These can be shown in diagrammatic form with one line showing the change in sales and underneath the level of profit generated.

Figure 13.1: The stages of the product life cycle

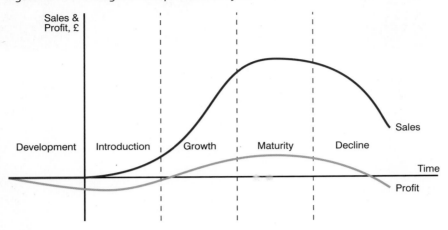

Stages of the product life cycle

Development – The product is not yet for sale but is being researched, developed and tested. The business will be investing with no immediate return. Market research and test marketing may be used to shape the development of the product. Promotion is likely to be restricted to press releases announcing the forthcoming launch.

Introduction – The product is launched and begins to sell; this may be to early adopters via a price skimming strategy; alternatively, introductory offers and penetration pricing strategies can be used to attract customers. There will commonly be heavy expenditure on promotion to build awareness and attract sales; the business is likely to be making a loss at this stage and cash flow will probably be negative.

Growth – Sales are increasing as the product becomes more well-known and a customer base is created. The marketing strategy may change emphasis, promotional activity may concentrate on building brand loyalty; prices may rise to premium level or fall to match the competition and grow market share. For the first time, cash flow moves into the positive; profits appear and then increase if this stage progresses as intended.

Maturity – Sales and profits are reaching their maximum level; average costs may begin to fall as economies of scale are achieved. Promotion may ease as the brand becomes established, with occasional campaigns to maintain sales or to differentiate it from rivals. Ideally the business wants to sustain the mature stage for as long as possible, it can use extension strategies (see below), but there will come a point when sales start to decline.

> **Economies of scale** are reductions in average cost brought about by an increase in output, e.g. by bulk-buying of raw materials.

Decline – The product is losing sales, newer and more innovative alternatives may have taken market share or customer preferences may have changed. Profits may still be made as long as the sales price exceeds the average cost. There will be little in the way of promotion at this stage; price is likely to be reduced to maintain some sales until the product reaches the end of its life. Once costs exceed revenues the product will be withdrawn from the market.

Activity

Try to think of real-life examples of products or services that would fit each stage of the product life cycle. Explain your choices.

Figure 13.2: Pricing and the product life cycle

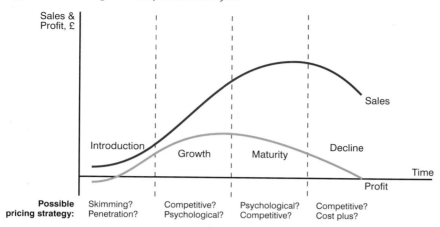

Extension strategies

An extension strategy is any method used to lengthen the maturity stage of the product life cycle by modifying the product, targeting a new market segment or promoting it in fresh ways. As the maturity stage is the most profitable stage in the life cycle, businesses will make every effort to prolong or extend this stage. When sales of a mature product begin to fall this indicates the potential for an extension strategy to halt the fall in sales or even to reach or surpass the former level.

Extension strategies involve changing elements of the marketing mix. They can include finding a new market or market segment for the product, finding new uses for the existing product, changing the appearance, format or packaging, developing variations of the original product or changing the pricing strategy and advertising. The effect of doing this on sales can be seen in Figure 13.3.

> An **extension strategy** is a way of prolonging or renewing the life cycle of a product, most commonly used during the mature stage of its life cycle.

Figure 13.3: The effect on sales of an extension strategy

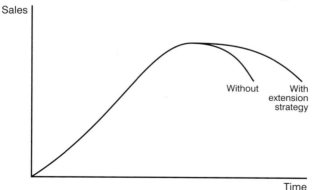

Product

The product can be changed in a major way or it can be subject to smaller changes, often evolving through a range of models, the iPhone is a good example of this. With each change the product is seen as being different. Existing customers may upgrade and new customers are attracted; the result is that the product continues to sell well and generate further profits for the company. The history of the Ford Fiesta illustrates this.

The Mars bar built a strong brand which was subsequently used for profitable additional products. In both cases there is undoubtedly an element of brand loyalty; some motorists will buy the new Fiesta just because it is a Fiesta, regardless of any improvements to the model, and many will buy a Mars ice cream because they like Mars bars. Nevertheless for both Ford and Mars the product life cycle has been successfully extended.

Promotion

The example of Lucozade is a classic study as to how clever promotion can extend the product life cycle. The emphasis shifted away from its use in illness and recovery and onto a different use in a different market segment. As more people began to find the time and inclination to follow sporting and leisure interests, there was a growing market for such a product. Lucozade launched a series of iconic adverts in the early 80s, featuring Olympic gold medal winner Daley Thompson, which reinforced the revised nature of the product to enhance sports performance. Since then it has become firmly established as one of the leading brands of energy and sporting drinks.

More recently, Kellogg's repositioned their soft-baked 'Nutri-Grain' bars away from daytime snacking to become a breakfast product, renaming them 'Nutri-Grain Morning Bars'. They now target people with 'no time for a proper breakfast', competing with market leader Belvita (Mondelez/Kraft) and others, in a market which they believe can continue to grow rapidly.

Boston Matrix and the product portfolio

Most businesses have a range of products to sell. This is known as the product portfolio. Some of these products will be best-sellers and generate large amounts of revenue; others may do less well, either because they are new or are no longer in demand. Business managers will want to know how each product is performing and to have a balanced portfolio. It may seem attractive to have nothing but best-sellers, but sooner or later these will be overtaken by better rivals and fade away. Good managers know that they need a flow of fresh new ideas coming from development to be the best-sellers of tomorrow.

The Boston Matrix is an analytical tool used by managers to look at both the actual and potential market share and growth of individual items in the product portfolio. It places products in four categories according to their market share and market growth.

Figure 13.4: The Boston Matrix

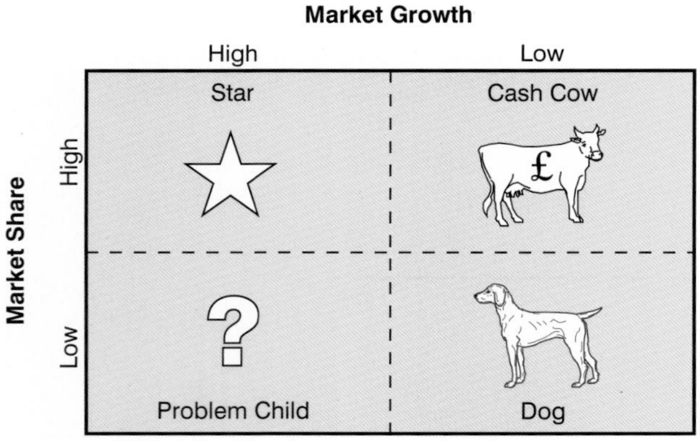

Stars have a high share of a high growth market.

Problem children or **Question marks** have a low share of a high growth market.

Cash cows have a large share of a slow growing or static market.

Dogs have a low share of a low growth market.

The idea is that the business will have products in each category, not just focus on one area. Those on the left hand side of the matrix are in the growth part of the product life cycle. Stars and Problem Children both have potential as their market is expanding, but they need to be promoted and protected. This will cost money and so Cash Cows are needed to generate the profits needed to support the stars and problem children that may become the future Cash Cows. Dogs are to be avoided but can be tolerated if they still contribute a little to profits. Having the right combination of product types is called a balanced portfolio.

An awareness of where each product is placed on the matrix can help with planning effective marketing strategies.

> The **Boston matrix** is a method of analysing a company's products in terms of their market share and growth potential.
>
> The **product portfolio** is the range of products that a business provides, sometimes called the product mix.

Rise and fall of the iPod

Apple launched the iPod with its distinctive click-wheel design and white bud headphones in 2001. It proved a massive success but 26 versions and 14 years later sales are 50% down year on year and further drops are expected. The people who would previously have bought iPods are now more likely to buy iPhones or iPads. When the iPhone was launched in 2007, Steve Jobs reportedly said that it was "the best iPod we've ever made."

Despite the major fall in sales, the iPod range still generates big revenues – $973m (£587m) in the last quarter, although by Apple's standards that is tiny compared to its total for all products over the same period of $57.6bn. "As long as the iPod can stay a quality product and not have them lose money, I really don't see any reason for them to kill it," argues Alex Heath, a writer for Cult of Mac.

Apple has just launched the Apple Watch and is said to have an Apple television on the way. Its biggest seller currently is the iPhone which accounts for over half of its revenue.

1. Which stages of the product life cycle would you place the iPhone, iPod, Apple Watch and the Apple television in? Explain your reasoning.

2. Which categories of the Boston Matrix would you place the iPhone, iPod and the Apple Mac into? Explain your reasoning.

3. Assess the usefulness of the product life cycle and the Boston matrix to Apple when examining their product portfolio.

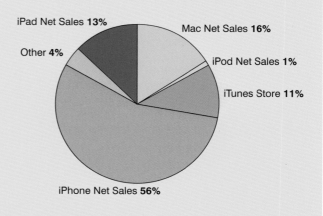

iPad Net Sales **13%**

Mac Net Sales **16%**

Other **4%**

iPod Net Sales **1%**

iTunes Store **11%**

iPhone Net Sales **56%**

Marketing strategies appropriate for different types of market

Mass markets
A mass marketing strategy ignores market segment differences and sets one strategy for the whole market. Mass marketing aims to attract all kinds of buyers by producing and distributing an attractive product at an attractive price.

A mass market involves large numbers of people. The wants of potential customers tend to be similar, the product or service is often standardised, heavily promoted and available over a wide area. Traditionally promotion has focused on radio, television, and newspapers to reach this broad customer base. Online promotion is now also reaching some mass markets. Reaching the largest possible audience and maximising exposure to the product is the target. Supermarkets, for example, cater for the mass market. Many of the people who see the advert may not be interested, but enough will be attracted to make it worthwhile. The total costs of mass marketing are high but the wide exposure brings down the cost per person.

Niche markets
Marketing strategies in niche markets are differentiated and specifically aimed at the niche segment of the market. Instead of casting a wide net as in mass marketing, niche marketing focuses on one particular section of the market that is likely to respond positively to a niche product or service.

Successful niche marketing depends on a good understanding of the needs and wants of potential customers in the niche category, without this knowledge marketing is unlikely to be successful. Once preferences are identified the strategy should focus on them. Price is less important in a niche market but the medium becomes more important as customers need to be precisely targeted, often via specialist publications, websites or social media groups. The cost per person will be higher than mass market but a higher success rate can make this worthwhile.

Business to business (B2B) and business to consumer (B2C) marketing
B2B and B2C are two contrasting types of selling. B2B, (business-to-business), is the process of selling products or services to business buyers for use in their companies. B2C, (business-to-consumer), entails selling directly to consumers who buy products or services for personal use.

There are some similarities in the marketing strategies used, in the sense that whether selling to consumers or to other businesses it is important to match products to the needs of the target market, at the right price and quality. However, there are some important differences.

B2C involves the customer directly engaging with the marketing and making their own spending decision. There is often emotional involvement as customers respond to promotion and advertising that can be heavily brand orientated. By contrast, the B2B approach should be more rational and focused on business goals rather than personal satisfaction. There will be promotion, but adverts are likely to appear in specialist trade magazines. Direct marketing and trade fairs are also common ways of establishing contact between businesses.

Marketing in B2B is often aimed at individuals who act as buyers for their organisations. There can be numerous meetings before a transaction occurs. The buyers may have to pass the decision to buy to senior managers or directors for final approval.

In B2C, consumers who buy products commonly pay a standard price. In B2B, price may vary by customer; those who can place large orders or negotiate special terms often pay lower prices than others. The product itself can be important, in terms of quality and also in the ability to deliver punctually or guarantee supply in the future.

Loyal customers tend to buy more and buy more regularly.

Consumer behaviour – how businesses develop customer loyalty

Selling more to existing buyers is easier, and cheaper, than finding new customers. Loyal customers tend to buy more, and buy more regularly; they will also recommend the business to others and so save promotional costs. Studies have shown that it costs 6 to 7 times more to acquire a new customer than to keep one. Ideas found in the previous sections can help to develop customer loyalty, such as effective promotion and a good brand image, but there are many other ways to create it as well.

Customer service – There is an old saying that 'The customer is king'. Appreciating the value of the customer and pleasing them is key to developing customer loyalty. Customers who feel valued, feel they receive good advice and find the service friendly are likely to be loyal and not buy elsewhere. A business's response when things go wrong is also important. Putting things right in an effective and caring way can turn a potential disaster into stronger customer loyalty.

> **Customer loyalty** means a preference for a product or brand, based on experience and/or an emotional attachment, which inclines buyers to repeat purchases and away from rivals.

> *News of bad customer service reaches more than twice as many ears as praise for a good service experience.*
>
> *For every customer who bothers to complain, nearly 26 others who are unhappy remain silent.*
>
> White House Office of Consumer Affairs

Loyalty cards and saver schemes – Such schemes have been around in the UK for over 40 years now, the UK loyalty card market is one of the most developed in the world. Many major chains operate some form of reward system. The most common form is the loyalty card where the purchaser presents the card and is either entitled to a discount there and then, or can accrue points or tokens to be used against future purchases. The idea is not new; since commerce first began tradesmen would look after regular customers with some discount or their best output. With numerous businesses competing for sales, the prospect of a few extra loyalty points can keep a consumer happy and ensure repeat business.

Exam style question

Tebay Motorway Services

Tebay is described as the UK's most popular motorway service station. There are two sites with unique facilities such as a duck pond, a farm shop, great views and a caravan park. In 1972 local farmers (the Dunnings) set it up. It is still locally owned and run, using a two or three stage distribution system with home-made and locally sourced food where possible.

Reviews are often glowing, with comments such as:

"I had the best service station lunch in history today."

"I'm not the only person who purposefully splits their journey to stop at Tebay."

"Tebay is amazing! How can a motorway stop be this good?"

"Quite an improvement on your typical Burger King and KFC combo… Forget the fried chicken or greasy chips at other services."

The owners know that if they stand still they will start to move backwards. They understand that to survive and thrive they must continue to innovate. Their latest development is to build a similar service station on the M5 near Gloucester. They describe themselves as anti-brands and see their local sourcing as part of their belief in what they do. They spend little on promotion.

Questions

1. What is meant by 'two or three stage distribution system'? *(2 marks)*

2. What is meant by 'brands'? *(2 marks)*

3. Explain likely priorities in Tebay's product design mix. *(4 marks)*

4. Explain the value of customer loyalty to Tebay. *(4 marks)*

5. Examine the suitability of *two* pricing strategies for Tebay. *(8 marks)*

6. Assess the decision to build a new service station around 200 miles from Tebay's original venture. *(10 marks)*

"A company's employees are its greatest asset and your people are your product."

Richard Branson

Staff as an asset; staff as a cost

Costco and Sam's Club

Costco is a membership-only warehouse club and is the second largest retailer in the United States. It focuses on selling products at low prices, often in large quantities. Its most recent sales figures showed a healthy 8% rate of growth. Costco workers start with an hourly wage of $11.50. An average Costco employee earns $21 an hour.

Walmart is the largest retailer in the US and the world, it also operates a membership scheme called Sam's club, similar to Costco, which only managed a 1.2% rise in sales. Walmart workers start with an hourly wage of $9.00. An average Walmart employee earns $13 an hour.

Costco also offers its employees opportunities for promotion and has lower worker turnover and far higher sales per employee than its rivals. Sales per employee at Costco are nearly double that at Sam's Club.

Why do you think Costco is willing to pay much higher wages than its rivals?

What are the advantages to Walmart in paying lower wages?

Why might 'lower worker turnover' be an advantage for Costco?

What other factors might explain the recent success of Costco?

In business an asset is defined as something of value, such as cash, equipment, inventory, or buildings, while a liability is defined as something that has a negative effect on the value of the business, such as a loan that must be repaid or outstanding invoices for supplies.

Managers like Richard Branson believe that its people are crucial to the success of a business and that looking after and valuing them is a priority. They believe in developing the skills of the existing staff so that their expertise can be used more effectively in developing the business, increasing productivity and profitability. People who feel valued are more likely to look after customers and to enhance the reputation of the business. Costco demonstrate that a well-treated workforce is more likely to be productive and cost effective in the long run.

Other businesses focus on staff as a major item of expenditure and as a large proportion of costs. Labour is seen as a cost to be kept as low as possible, for example by paying the minimum wage or arrangements such as zero-hours contracts. For some businesses, even this can be undercut by 'outsourcing' production overseas to take advantage of cheaper foreign labour. This has been the trend in many manufacturing industries over the last few decades. China has grown to become the world's second largest economy in this time, mainly by having a plentiful supply of cheap labour which western businesses have used in order to minimise production costs and increase competitiveness.

Outsourcing

Outsourcing is when business tasks or processes are undertaken by an external provider rather than within the business. This can involve the manufacturing of components or whole products and services such as IT provision, accountancy or maintenance. This allows the original business to concentrate on its core activities and is usually more cost-effective and efficient than doing everything themselves. The business taking on the outsourcing will have the relevant expertise and resources, tasks can be completed faster and with better quality output. A good working relationship between the businesses is essential; problems can arise if communications break down.

Many businesses outsource services such as accountancy and window cleaning to local specialist providers. Some outsource major aspects, such as production of what they sell, across the world. In garment manufacture, for example, producers in China, Bangladesh and other Asian countries have far lower costs than Western European businesses. Manufacture of electronic products, footwear, toys and many other products is now concentrated in Asia. Whilst reduction of costs is the prime consideration here, outsourcing also increases flexibility of operations.

> **Outsourcing** is the name for shifting activity away from an original producer, often to lower cost suppliers. Early outsourcing was often for services such as cleaning or payroll preparation. In many cases, goods designed in developed countries are now produced in low-wage developing countries.

Flexible workforce

A flexible workforce is one that can adapt quickly to changing circumstances. The opposite extreme is a rigid system in which people stick to the single task they are responsible for and clock on and off from work at the same set times in each working day. This was once the norm in many manufacturing industries, nowadays greater flexibility is widely seen as desirable.

Multi-skilling

One aspect of flexibility involves workers being able to perform different tasks and move from one area of operations to another. In competitive markets, having a flexible and responsive workforce can be very valuable. It helps the business to compete effectively, by being able to respond quickly to changing market conditions and to limit labour costs by requiring fewer specialists.

> **Multi-skilling** is the practice of training employees to develop the ability to do more than one task, or of recruiting employees who can do several different things.

Many businesses see the extra training costs of extending what workers can do as a valuable investment. There are several advantages: staff absences can be covered easily without loss of production, the business can respond to sudden changes in demand and special orders can be catered for. Many workers enjoy variety in what they do and feel more valued when trusted with more tasks, so their motivation can benefit.

Part-time and temporary working

It is inflexible for many businesses to have only full-time and permanent staff. For seasonal businesses such as tourism and agriculture, staff needed vary through the year. Supermarkets, fast-food outlets and many shops have irregular patterns of demand through the week, with very busy periods when demand is high and other times when there are hardly any customers. A fixed number of all full-time staff may mean that there are not enough helpers available at peak periods and that there is little to keep workers occupied during the quiet times.

Part-time and temporary work allow more people to be brought in to match the busy periods, matching staff levels with peaks and troughs to maximise efficiency and minimise costs. This can also be beneficial for some workers who may not want a permanent full time job; parents with school-age children or students for example.

Recent years have seen a growth in the numbers of zero-hours contracts where the employer is not obliged to provide the worker with any minimum working hours, and the worker is (normally) not obliged to accept the hours offered. Currently, some large businesses such as Sports Direct and Wetherspoon make extensive use of such contracts. The worker often has to wait for a call when the employer gets busy. For many workers the insecurity in this kind of employment is worrying, but supporters of the contracts like the flexibility that they can offer. In early 2015 the ONS estimated the number of UK zero-hours contracts to be 1.4 million.

Advantages and disadvantages of zero-hours contracts

Advantages	Disadvantages
To the employer: Flexibility to respond to fluctuating demand for their product. Less costly employment rights for workers.	**To the employer:** Workers possibly less committed and motivated.
To the employee: Some employees value the flexibility.	**To the employee:** Less income. 2014 average £188 per week, nearly £300 below full-time (TUC data). Little financial stability and security, and e.g. hard to get credit cards or mortgages. Fewer rights, e.g. to maternity pay, sick pay or redundancy.

Flexible hours and home working

In 2014 a new law gave all employees with 26 weeks or more service the right to request flexible working, which employers must address in a 'reasonable manner'. Some employers have identified 'core' hours and allowed flexibility outside those times. Any flexibility is difficult in some situations; production lines depend on continuity between stages, for example.

> **Flexible hours** often means that employees are expected to work a certain number of hours in a given time period but there are not fully set times when they have to be at their workplace.

An employee could start and finish earlier or later, perhaps even working an hour or two extra each day so can they take a day off occasionally or simply avoid rush hour travel. This system is sometimes called flexi-time.

The number of employees working from home in office-type jobs, or using home as a base from which to travel for their work, is steadily increasing. Homeworking can cover a variety of arrangements, ranging from working entirely at home apart from occasional meetings, through splitting time between office and home to working mainly in the office and from home only occasionally.

Advantages to the employee are the reduced time and cost of commuting and greater potential to fit work around other lifestyle requirements. The employer can save expenditure on office space and other overheads. Trust is required that the employee will work efficiently without supervision, though it is actually not unusual for productivity to increase away from workplace distractions. Working from home can be lonely without the company of fellow workers and of course the home needs to be equipped as a workspace as well. Modern communications have undoubtedly helped homeworking to be a more popular

Flexible working entails movements away from fixed tasks, working hours and locations.

and practical option. A downside here is that smartphones and laptops can make it hard to escape from pressures of work.

> **Flexible working** entails movements away from fixed tasks, working hours and locations. For many businesses this allows greater ability to vary their way of working whilst also controlling their costs. Greater flexibility for employees must sometimes be set against reduced security for their work and income.

Think!

Would you prefer a flexible working arrangement or traditional fixed hours?

What would be the strengths and disadvantages of each of these for you?

Distinction between dismissal and redundancy

In everyday language, when people are dismissed they are sacked. A dismissal has to be fair and correct procedures must be followed. If an employee feels they have been unfairly dismissed, legal proceedings can be started and an employment tribunal may hear the case. A summary dismissal is when someone is dismissed instantly without notice or pay in lieu of notice, usually because of gross misconduct (e.g. theft, fraud or violence).

Redundancy can be voluntary or compulsory. Once employees have been with a business for two years they are entitled to redundancy payments if no longer wanted. Rather than force people to lose their jobs, a business may ask for volunteers to accept redundancy. This often comes with some extra payment attached and may appeal to those wanting to retire early or become self-employed. With both types of redundancy there are required procedures to be followed.

This is not the fault of the employee and may happen for a number of reasons. Mergers and takeovers often result in duplication of resources and rationalisation within the new organisation means some jobs are no longer needed. When Aviva took over Friends Life in early 2015 there were 1500 jobs lost. The business may simply be failing or having to respond to lower demand in a recession. New machinery, automation or outsourcing sometimes mean less labour is needed.

Dismissal means a worker is required to leave the job because their behaviour is unsatisfactory or they have repeatedly failed to work to the required standard.

Redundancy happens when a worker is told to leave the job because their skills are no longer of use to the organisation.

Employer/employee relationships

Employer/employee relations refer to the communication and discussion that takes place directly between an individual and employer (the individual approach) and between representatives of employees and employers (collective bargaining). Discussions will mostly centre on areas such as pay, the working environment and conditions, hours, production levels, working procedures and health & safety.

It may seem that the interests of the two sides are opposed. Employers are concerned with the level of profits so want to keep costs down, whereas employees want a good level of pay and good working conditions and terms. Yet without the co-operation and motivation of the workforce the employer will not necessarily have a long term future and the employees know that without the continued success of the business there will be no jobs.

Disputes do arise and can at times be acrimonious. However, in most situations employees and employers know that they share a common interest in the success of their business. The relationships between them are often harmonious and positive.

Collective bargaining

When employees' representatives get together with owners or managers to discuss workplace issues this is called collective bargaining. The workforce is often represented by a trade union. If an agreement is reached it is called a collective agreement. If not, in extreme cases the union may undertake industrial action which covers a variety of tactics from work-to-rule (working slowly and adhering to all procedures) to a strike (withdrawal of labour).

Prolonged disputes may be referred to ACAS (The Advisory, Conciliation and Arbitration Service) a public and impartial body set up to help resolve such difficulties. By contrast with the large scale disputes of the past, its role today is more of an advisory and training body which tries to prevent disputes arising in the first place. Strikes are now unusual and only likely to occur when relationships have seriously broken down.

Casual labour

A report from the TUC (Trades Union Congress) has revealed an increased spread of low-paid, insecure and casual work across the British economy since the financial crash of 2008.

In 2008, one in 20 men and one in 16 women worked in the casual labour market. Today, according to the TUC, one in 12 of all workers is in uncertain and temporary employment, which includes zero-hours contracts.

Casual labour market	2008	2014
Men	655,000	1,060,000
Women	795,000	1,080,000

Why might the number of casual employees have increased so much since 2008?

What are the advantages for employers of using casual labour?

Are there any disadvantages for the employers?

What are the advantages and disadvantages for the employees?

Chapter 15

Recruitment, selection and training

You have just interviewed two candidates for a new executive position. One of them is young, friendly, keen to succeed, enthusiastic about joining your business and made a positive impression. However she has no experience in this particular line of work. The other is older and well qualified with a successful track record of this work in other businesses, yet she did not interview that well and seemed rather withdrawn and noncommittal.

What are the advantages and disadvantages of appointing either of these candidates?

Which one would you choose and why?

Recruitment and selection process

When the need for extra or replacement staff arises, businesses need to find applicants. They can do this internally or externally.

> **Internal recruitment** means that potential applicants are found within the organisation.
>
> **External recruitment** means that potential candidates are found from outside the organisation, either by advertising or using recruitment agencies.

If a business recruits internally it is usually quicker and cheaper than having to advertise or wait for external recruitment agencies to find some suitable applicants. Someone from inside the business will already be familiar with the way the business works, which will save on training time and costs. Managers will know the applicants and have a good understanding of their capabilities and qualities, rather than having to rely on references and interviews. For the existing staff the possibility of internal promotion can be a motivating factor and increase productivity.

Despite its apparent advantages there are drawbacks to internal recruitment. The number of applicants will be limited by the size of the business and the number of potential candidates with the ability to fill the post. With a wider range of external candidates to choose from, a better and more capable applicant may be found. Even if a suitable internal candidate is available, their promotion leaves another vacancy to be filled.

Using a recruiting agency (sometimes called 'head-hunters') can be the best way to recruit, particularly for executive or specialist positions. They will have access to a wide range of possible candidates who may be more skilled or experienced than internal applicants. Recruiting agencies are also used for less specialist staff such as temporary office workers or cleaners. However, using an outside agency is likely to be more expensive and time consuming and is not guaranteed to produce the right candidate; references can be inaccurate and impressions at interview misleading.

There is an old business saying – *"Recruit for attitude, train for skills"*

Reasons for recruiting for a positive attitude…

- If applicants are young they will not have existing skills or experience anyway.
- If working relationships are important and recruits have to work within a team.
- If dealing with customers or clients is an important aspect of the job.
- If the business values openness and the ability to adapt.

Reasons for recruiting for skill...

● If the job demands a level of technical competence without which it cannot be done.

● If training in the skills is very expensive or time consuming.

● If experience is an important aspect of the job.

Of course, many jobs require a mixture of the two. A business may be impressed by a new accountant who is enthusiastic, committed and able to form positive working relationships with other staff. However, without formal accountancy qualifications that recruit is unlikely to be appointed.

Interviews

An interview meeting is often a key part of the selection process, despite the time and costs involved if several candidates are seen. Whether or not someone's 'face fits' is essentially a subjective judgement. Evidence suggests that such judgements are often made quickly, perhaps just on a first impression. That someone is clean, tidy, and polite and smiling at interview is reassuring but not much of a guide to future performance. In defence of such flimsy assessment, its supporters argue that references frequently flatter applicants, ignoring weaknesses, and qualifications give little indication of how someone will perform.

Think!

When you first meet someone, what in their appearance and attitudes will have a positive impact on you?

How might you set out to make a positive impression on someone when you first meet them?

In many cases, psychological tests or practical tasks are now combined with interviews. However, this increases the costs involved so is used more in recruiting for skilled and senior roles where mistakes can be most damaging.

Cost of recruitment and training

Recruitment and training are expensive processes. The cost of labour turnover (replacing an employee) has been estimated to be up to 150% of the employees' remuneration package (pay). A survey of 610 CEOs

An interview meeting is often a key part of the selection process.

by Harvard Business School estimated that typical mid-level managers require 6.2 months to reach the break-even point where they start to make a net positive contribution to the business.

Recruitment is just the first step in the process; once the right person is in place, businesses need to provide adequate training so the new employee can do the work and start producing for the company.

Costs can be divided into two groups. So called 'hard costs' include: advertising costs, recruitment agency costs, interview expenses, time spent dealing with applications and interviewing. For senior appointments, there may be removal expenses and even a 'Golden hello' (a payment or bonus to encourage someone to work for you). Then there are the training and induction costs, needed to get the new employee up to speed and familiar with the work and the company culture.

On top of that there are the 'soft costs', which are difficult to quantify but still affect the business. There will be a loss of production when staff are involved in recruitment and training. Also it takes time for new staff to build up the knowledge and experience that their predecessor had. It also takes time to build up good new working relationships.

> The costs of recruitment help to explain why many businesses use arbitrary systems to reject many applicants, giving no consideration to even potentially valuable employees.
>
> Some businesses stop opening applications once they have seen 'enough'.
>
> Some use very strict limits on qualifications, age, gender and ethnicity, even when this breaks laws against discrimination.
>
> One local employer refuses to even open application letters which have gone through a stamping machine, preferring to consider only people who appear to have paid for their own stamp.

Low labour turnover

> **Labour turnover** measures the rate at which a business loses staff. They may or may not need replacing.

High labour turnover can be a problem because there will be recruitment costs for replacing staff. There will be a loss of know-how and customer goodwill and a potential loss of sales. Productivity will be lower as new staff will need time for training and may not be as skilled as more experienced staff. The problems become worse if a culture of impermanence develops, with people unsure of who or what will change next.

Low labour turnover is generally considered to be an advantage because recruitment and training costs are lower and there is less disruption to production. It can be an indicator of contented and therefore well-motivated employees. However, low labour turnover may mean that the business does not get the benefit of fresh ideas, new energy or a questioning attitude towards established (and possibly stale) ways of doing things. It can also mean that your employees lack ambition and are really not as productive as they could be.

Types of training

Training is the key to creating an efficient workforce and this is particularly important for new staff. 'Investors in People', funded by the UK government, aims to help businesses to get the best from their training and staff. It operates an accreditation system to encourage and recognise good practice. Its 2015 employee sentiment poll, for example, found that more than half of all employees were considering changing their jobs, so advice was offered on how to handle this potentially disruptive issue.

Induction

Induction is the training given to new employees to familiarise them with the work environment, the requirements of the job and their colleagues. Induction training should be the first stage of an ongoing training programme and should help new employees to become effective quickly and help to improve motivation and performance. Areas covered will vary depending on the job but will include everyday needs such as toilet and canteen facilities, office procedures, where everything is and who to ask for help. The only legal requirement is to cover any relevant health and safety requirements.

On-the-job

As might be expected from the description, this involves training in the workplace. A new employee learns about the job by watching and then doing whilst under supervision. In its most basic form it is sometimes called 'sitting next to Nellie' which means following and working alongside an existing worker to learn the skills needed for a particular process. More sophisticated methods will involve a mentoring process with a trained and experienced person responsible for a planned training programme.

The main advantage of on-the-job training is that it is cheaper than sending people on courses run by outside organisations. While the employee is learning they are at least being partly productive and the training is directly suited to their future role. On the other hand, the training may not be ideal; an experienced worker may be very proficient at their job but not have the teaching skills needed to properly train newcomers. Businesses may not have the internal skills necessary to cover new areas such as implementing new legislation or using high tech equipment.

Off-the-job

Training takes place away from the immediate workplace. This might be at a specialist training centre, or at a company's own premises. Many colleges run courses in skills relevant to major local industries. This type of training can be particularly useful for developing transferable skills that can be used in many different parts of the business. It can be used as part of a broad induction programme. Such training is likely to be professional with good resourcing and may result in professional and transferable qualifications. The main drawback of course is the cost, not just in direct payments to the training provider but also in productive time lost while the employee attends the course.

Many training schemes involve elements of both on and off-the-job such as apprenticeships where the apprentice spends most of the time in the workplace but also attends a local college on a regular basis. Teacher training students alternate between blocks of time at University and in the classroom on teaching practice.

> **On-the-job training** means learning in the workplace. This is central to many apprenticeships, for example.
>
> **Off-the-job training** takes employees away from normal working tasks to focus on required learning. This can be delivered by outside agencies or by trainers from within the business.

Continuing training

The demands of evolving technology, and the desire for multi-skilling, help to explain why training can be a lifelong process of development. Even if an employee has a stable role which she/he has mastered, stepping away from the job and thinking about how things are done can be valuable. Many businesses now use annual appraisals of performance and development in which the identification of suitable additional training plays an important part. This can help with motivation and with preparation for internal promotions.

Chapter 16

Organisational design

Structure

Organisations are structured in differing ways and each will have their own individual corporate culture or way of doing things. These have a great influence on the way the business works and directly affect its efficiency and competitiveness. Three key aspects of operations are strongly influenced by the structure. These are effectiveness of communication, clarity of responsibilities and motivation of staff.

Some aspects of the culture may not be formally recorded, having evolved over time. The organisational structure will be more formal, defining where authority and responsibility lie, who each person is accountable to and the ways by which communication should pass through the business. Effective organisational structures make working relationships easier and so help businesses to reach their objectives. Communication and order will be maintained yet the organisation can still be flexible and creative. This combination should increase efficiency.

An **organisational structure** is the framework, usually hierarchical, which shows how a business arranges its lines of authority and communications, and allocates responsibilities and duties.

There is no single best structure; different approaches suit different businesses. What is clear is that the wrong organisational structure will restrict the performance of the business. Getting it right means considering what is going to be most effective and then adapting the organisation to meet its own objectives successfully.

Hierarchy and chain of command

A hierarchy is a system where employees are ranked in layers one above the other. Each higher level has fewer employees than the one below, typically in a pyramid shape. There will be a **chain of command**, so that information and decisions can be communicated from one line manager to another and so on down through the layers. Each individual will have responsibilities to others both above and below them in the hierarchy. Hierarchical structures are found in many organisations.

A small business, say one owned by a sole trader, might simply have the one 'boss' with everyone else answering to her or him. Larger organisations tend to have a longer chain of command, think for example of an army with successive levels of officers above non-commissioned officers such as sergeants and corporals and then ordinary soldiers.

Span of control

At each stage in a chain of command, one person has a number of employees directly under them. The senior person 'controls' those who are below her/him, the subordinates are directly answerable upwards.

The span of control refers to the number of subordinates directly answerable to someone at the next level of responsibility.

A wide span of control can create problems if there are so many subordinates that the manager can't supervise all of them closely enough. On the other hand, where employees are given more independence and responsibility with less close supervision, they may react positively, welcoming greater freedom and showing readiness to work hard.

A narrow span of control, with less subordinates at each level, has its strengths and weaknesses. It allows close supervision, particularly useful if subordinates have unproven ability or poor motivation. Against this, feeling a lack of trust and being intensely supervised can be a cause of poor motivation. Another issue here is that people at the bottom of a many layered pyramid can become quite remote from those at the top. Communication through many layers can prove difficult. The best approach depends on the circumstances and the people involved.

> A **chain of command** is the official hierarchy of authority in an organisation, setting out the sequence of responsibility for giving and taking instruction.
>
> The **span of control** is the measure of how many people are directly answerable to each person in a chain of command

Centralised and decentralised

Centralisation means businesses have a structure that keeps all decision-making at the top of the hierarchy, usually in the (central) head office. The most senior management keeps close control on what goes on throughout the business. For example, businesses such as McDonalds are centralised so that control and standardisation can be maintained in all their many branches.

With a centralised structure it is easier to maintain an overall strategic direction, decision making is easier and more rapid and can be quickly passed down the structure. Budgeting and finance can be more easily co-ordinated and implemented. By standardising everything it may be possible to achieve economies of scale (lower average costs) and increase efficiency. A centralised structure works best with strong leadership, in uncertain economic times this can be a real advantage.

Drawbacks to a centralised structure are that it can be rather bureaucratic and lack flexibility. Rather than being able to respond quickly to local problems in the branches, it can take time for information to be fed back to head office and then managers to meet and make a decision. Even then, the decision may not be a well-informed one. Local managers are likely to best understand local issues, needs and opportunities, but might not be able to show head office how their situation is best dealt with. One possible result is that poor decisions are made, with local managers left feeling powerless and demotivated.

Figure 16.1: Centralisation and decentralisation

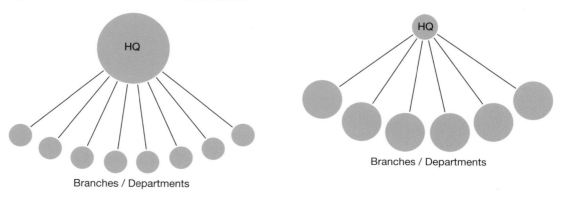

By contrast, decentralisation means moving the decision making process away from a central head office and spreading it throughout the organisation, often to branch level. Decentralisation is closely linked with delegation. Delegation involves giving individuals greater responsibility for decision making, rather than having central managers handing down all decisions to employees who simply carry out instructions. For example, Tesco allows its branch managers to make many decisions without needing to consult Head Office. The idea is that decisions will be taken as close as possible to where they are going to be put into effect.

With decentralisation, senior managers in head office are free to concentrate on the most important strategic decisions, as the other everyday decisions can be made further down the organisational structure. People lower down the chain have a greater understanding of the market and their customers and can react faster to local changes. This may enable them to make more effective decisions than senior managers. Giving responsibility to local managers is a form of empowerment which can increase motivation.

The very act of decentralising and delegation also creates potential problems. It can be more difficult to co-ordinate overall strategy, so different parts of the business may pull in different ways.

Communications may be more complicated without a clear, strong chain of command and can break down. There can be a lack of accountability if things go wrong, so people can feel pushed towards covering their own backs by passing blame to others. Economies of scale are less easy to achieve if local managers have control of what is stocked or sold in their branches. Competent managers are not available in unlimited supply, so having more decision makers can increase the chances of some poor decisions being made. It may sometimes be the case that employees at branch level do not want the extra responsibility and are more comfortable being told what to do.

Centralisation entails concentrating power at head office and normally at the top of the hierarchy. Standard approaches and policies are applied throughout the business.

Decentralisation means delegating responsibility to local mangers so that they can make decisions appropriate for their local conditions.

Types of structure

Figure 16.2: Tall and flat spans of control

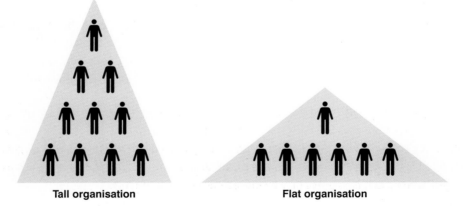

Tall organisation   Flat organisation

Tall

Tall hierarchical organisations are sometimes associated with autocratic leadership styles as there are clear lines of authority and control is concentrated at the top of the chain. A tall structure will have narrower spans of control meaning that each employee is closely supervised and decisions cascade down from the leader at the top. With more layers, there are more managers so greater specialisation becomes possible.

Roles and responsibilities tend to be clearly defined, giving a sense of purpose and order. Employees in the lower parts of the hierarchy can see a clear path for promotions which can be a motivating factor for those frustrated by close supervision.

Flat

A flatter hierarchy may be preferred when businesses are trying to become more flexible and responsive to changing market conditions. Or there may be pressure to cut costs, in which case it would be helpful to have fewer people on managerial salaries. Either way, delayering may be considered. Delayering involves reducing the number of levels within an organisational hierarchy. It usually entails increasing a managers' average span of control. It reshapes the structure from a tall pyramid to a much flatter shape.

There does seem to be a trend towards flatter structures, which may be connected to the importance of good, rapid communications in present day businesses. Quick, clear decision making and a willingness to listen to employees' ideas and suggestions can be key factors in the ability of the business to react swiftly to market change.

Delayering flattens an organisational hierarchy by removing levels of management.

Delayering examples

In 2011 the BBC (British Broadcasting Organisation) announced a 'Quality First' plan which would reduce the hierarchy of its workforce to seven levels from the previous nine. Besides hopefully leading to better decisions, this entailed reducing the number of managers and reducing the need for office space. By 2011, the future income of the BBC from TV licencing was uncertain.

Airline Flybe had been badly hit by recession, by 2012-13 losses had risen to over £40 million for the financial year. A mix of delayering and downsizing turned this round to a profit of £8.1m in 2013-14.

In 2014 the Aviva insurance group delayered by removing a regional management level between operations in each country and head office. Perhaps more logically, countries were divided between two groups: the slower growing developed countries and the faster changing countries with more potential growth.

Why is delayering often seen when businesses are struggling?

When might a successful business delayer?

Matrix structures

In a matrix, individuals belong to groups according to their speciality (such as design or operations control) and work in teams on specific projects. Teams that cut across specialities can benefit from empowerment and creativity in combining their ideas. This can give valuable flexibility to an organisation. A matrix approach is particularly suited to creative organisations in fast changing markets, such as Google. Once a project is complete, employees may be moved onto a different team.

Individuals in a matrix structure often have more than one manager, for example an accountant may be part of the finance department and so responsible to the finance manager, whilst also assigned to work on a specific project such as building a new production line where she might also be responsible to the project manager. This can create ambiguity and potential confusion, unless there is a clear way of working which is managed carefully. More stable or traditional organisations might have less to gain from a matrix approach, though this could be a good way to shake up a business stuck in a rut. Team leaders have to take responsibility for managing their projects, this can offer people the opportunity to experience management roles but there is a risk of errors being made.

> A **tall organisational structure** has many levels of responsibility, often combined with relatively small spans of control.
>
> A **flat organisational structure** has fewer levels, often combined with larger spans of control and more delegation.
>
> A **matrix structure** combines departmental organisation with teams formed from across departments to undertake specific projects.

Impact of different organisational structures on business

Picture a manufacturing plant where a production line mass produces a standard item. Many of the jobs involved are unskilled. This is a context in which 'scientific management' on Taylors lines (next page) might be seen as appropriate. There could well be a centralised approach with a rigid chain of command and careful supervision. In contemporary Britain, there might be reliance on casual labour and perhaps zero hours contracts, with little need to train staff who are seen as there solely for their pay.

Figure 16.3: A caricature structure

This is a caricature structure which might once have existed. However, if such simple jobs as are envisaged above have not now been automated they may instead have been outsourced to a country with lower wages. In the vast majority of jobs people can make an important difference so setting an environment in which they can thrive is important.

People like to be trusted and respected, most of them like to take some responsibility and many of them like to work in teams. Training and personal development are attractive to many of us. The caricature plant above offered little in these terms and such a plant would probably now be working at a competitive disadvantage compared to rival producers.

Many organisations have grown in relatively haphazard ways, often seeking to meet immediate priorities without working to a long term vision of how the organisation can best be structured for the future. Questioning and realigning structures can have great value, but is often only considered when a business faces a crisis (as in the case of Flybe).

Although they have attractions, a matrix structure might be inappropriate for many activities and flexible working hours might be difficult where work processes are integrated. All managements face the challenge of combining effective communication, clear responsibilities and getting the best from their people with flexibility as the business situation evolves. There is no universal right approach. Managers must decide what is best for their organisation and hope that their choices put them in a strong position compared to their rivals.

Motivation in theory and practice

The importance of employee motivation to a business

Motivating employees is vital for any business that wants to maximise efficiency. Motivated people are likely to work harder and be more concerned with the success of what they do. This can mean that they are more careful and conscientious in their work, which will improve quality and reduce waste. They will interact more positively with customers, creating loyalty and encouraging repeat purchases. They will be happier in their work and are less likely to leave, which reduces the costs of replacement and re-training. Motivated people are more likely to communicate with managers and suggest improvements and solutions to problems. All of this can create a competitive advantage and increase profitability.

Motivation theories

Much has been written on how to create a motivated workforce. Key thinkers in this area include Taylor, Mayo, Maslow and Herzberg. Psychologists have played a significant part in developing ideas on motivation. Their work often builds on common sense and their view of human nature.

Think!

In any group of workers, students or others, there are likely to be variations in the strength of motivation.

Why do you think some people and some groups have stronger motivation?

When your motivation varies, what makes it stronger or weaker?

Taylor (scientific management)

Frederick Taylor formed his ideas in the early 20th century by observing people at work. He believed that by careful and scientific observation, a job could be broken down into its component parts so that the most efficient way of doing it could be calculated. This led to an 'ideal' level of production per worker. Taylor (and 'Taylorism') believed that all workers were motivated by money and so if more was produced a bonus was earned, if less was produced then earnings were lost.

Figure 17.1: How Taylor's ideas worked...

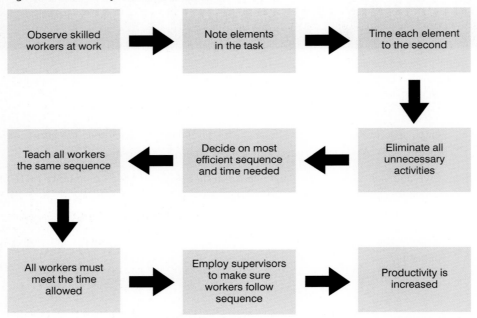

Taylor's scientific approach was not universally popular or successful; workers became worried that if they were more productive there might be job losses as fewer workers were needed. The work became more monotonous and boring. Attempting to reach targets and trigger bonuses led to mistakes being made and quality suffering. To maintain quality and efficiency more supervision was needed. Taylor assumed that all workers could work at the same rate and that money was the sole motivating factor. These simplifications were unrealistic but costs were cut in some cases.

Despite the problems, Taylor's scientific management theories changed the way much work was done and they became a starting point for subsequent ideas on motivation.

> **Scientific management** entailed detailed analysis of work processes to find the most efficient methods. Money was seen as the only motivator for workers.

Mayo (human relations theory)

In time, this rather mechanistic thinking was superseded by the **human relations approach**. During the 1930s, some business research suggested that employees would be more productive if they were treated as individuals, encouraged to communicate and to work as a team.

> The **human relations approach** emphasises the importance of the ways in which people interact and how they are treated. Motivation can improve when the employee feels more involved.

Elton Mayo was a psychologist and a Harvard researcher. He was involved in some early motivation experiments at Western Electric's Hawthorne plant where they varied environmental factors such as lighting and temperature to see if it affected productivity. To their frustration they discovered that increasing the lighting and reducing the lighting had the same effect; they both increased output. What had changed to bring this about was that the group reacted positively to being observed and involved. This became known as 'The Hawthorne effect'.

Mayo concluded that psychological and social factors played a larger role in productivity than the physical elements put forward by the proponents of scientific management. Later research led Mayo to emphasise the importance of the group, its social aspects and the importance of communication as a two way process and not just from boss to worker. This was the start of the human relations approach.

The human relations approach works well when employees and managers feel they are working towards common goals. Over the years a range of theories has developed. In practice, managers use a combination of approaches to develop motivational strategies that best suit the individual business.

Maslow (hierarchy of needs)

Abraham Maslow (1908-70) was a psychologist who believed that people had a whole set of needs that must be fulfilled in order for them to be motivated. These needs also had to be met in order of priority.

He illustrated this with a pyramid – people start by fulfilling their more basic needs at the base of the pyramid. Once those are satisfied they move up to the next set of needs and then, layer by layer to the top. Motivation comes from a person's desire to satisfy each of these needs and move on to the next level. The higher up on the pyramid the more complex the needs become.

Figure 17.2: Maslow's hierarchy of needs

Needs	What they mean
Self-actualisation	Fulfilling potential, being able to develop and be creative, making things happen, being the best that you can be. This stage brings full satisfaction with work and life.
Self-esteem	Gaining recognition for achievements at work, praise and promotion. The feeling that an individual is achieving something and contributing to group success.
Social needs	Interacting with work colleagues, making friendships and relationships and team-working. A feeling of belonging somewhere and being part of a group.
Safety needs	A safe working environment and job security, knowing that there will be employment and security not just now but also in the future
Basic physical needs	These are the needs considered essential to maintain life – food, drink and shelter. Businesses satisfy these needs by paying wages that enable workers to pay the bills.

Maslow's approach saw meeting people's needs as essential to motivation, with motivation stronger at the higher levels of his **hierarchy**.

In many ways this is an attractive, simple and useful model which businesses can use. For example, systems for recognising and praising good work can add valuably to self-esteem.

Job satisfaction does not necessarily mean that a worker will become more highly motivated or productive.

However, there are some problems with it. Maslow said that each level has to be satisfied before moving on to the next but this is not always the case. For example, voluntary charity workers may reach the top levels but not be able to satisfy their basic needs without a wage, or a promotion may only be temporary, so that safety needs are not being met. It is also the case that individual behaviour seems to respond to several needs at once, not just one. It can be difficult to decide when a level has actually been reached or fulfilled and job satisfaction does not necessarily mean that a worker will become more highly motivated or productive.

Herzberg (two factor theory)

Herzberg first published his theory in 1959 in a book entitled 'The Motivation to Work'. He based his ideas on in-depth interviews with over two hundred employees, having asked them what pleased and displeased them about their work. He found that the factors causing job satisfaction (which led to motivation) were different to those that caused dissatisfaction.

Frederick Herzberg was also a psychologist and there are some similarities between his and Maslow's theories: both argued that certain needs must be satisfied in order to motivate people. Based on his findings Herzberg took this point further and argued that it was not just the motivating factors such as praise and promotion that were needed but also the 'absence' of the other factors that would lead to dissatisfaction (if not improved), for example, poor working conditions or low pay.

He called these Hygiene Factors – they do not motivate by themselves but if they aren't up to standard, dissatisfaction might occur. Before motivation can even begin, the Hygiene Factors must be seen to. Putting these factors right before attempting to use the Motivation Factors is important, otherwise employees will not respond to managers' attempts to motivate them.

Motivating Factors	• Personal achievement • Stimulating work • Status	• Responsibility • Praise and recognition • Promotion	These will encourage motivation **but only** if Hygiene Factors are satisfied first
Hygiene factors	• Working conditions • Pay levels • Company policy	• Job security • Closeness of supervision • Relations with co-workers	If Hygiene Factors are not on a sufficiently high level, motivation will remain weak

Herzberg separated positive **motivating factors** from **hygiene factors** that weaken motivation and can block the impact of motivating factors.

ATS Tyres

In 2008 tyre retailer ATS was making a financial loss, the worker engagement score measured commitment to the business at below 30% and staff turnover was 40%. The new HR director, Irene Stark, was given the job of helping the business return to profit.

She realised that ATS had to alter employees' attitudes and the way they worked. She decided that one of the best ways to do this was to make sure staff were aware of everything that was going on in the organisation.

"We told staff what was going on and treated them like adults," she said. "Some of them didn't even know we were losing money."

Irene and her team involved staff in drawing up a three-year business plan, and then communicated the plan to all employees. All staff were given a face-to-face briefing by their line manager. A programme of learning and development initiatives was also started.

By 2013 the employee engagement score was over 60%, staff turnover had fallen to 16% a year, compared with 40% five years before, customer complaints had reduced and ATS had returned to profit.

Using your knowledge of motivational theory explain why Irene's ideas were so successful.

Why did Irene not just offer higher wages to improve motivation?

Explain why lower staff turnover and reduced customer complaints might have helped ATS to return to profit.

Would Irene's ideas have worked for all businesses? Explain your answer.

Financial incentives to improve employee performance

Money is not the only basis on which people choose their jobs, but we all find it useful. Linking pay to performance is widely seen as an effective way to improve motivation and achievement. The basic assumption is that staff performance will improve if there is a monetary reward for reaching an agreed target.

Financial incentives range from individual piecework schemes to the so-called 'fat-cat' bonuses of city traders.

Piecework

Piecework means that each production worker gets paid according to their quantity of output. An agreed payment is set for each item produced. The more that the worker produces the more they earn; there is an incentive to be as productive as possible. One main drawback is that the quality of the work may suffer as workers try to get as much done as possible.

Commission

A commission payment is usually based on a percentage of business generated by an employee such as a salesperson and is used as an incentive to increase worker productivity. A commission may be paid in addition to basic salary or instead of a salary. Employees can often take salary pay for granted but knowing that extra effort or results means more pay can motivate.

Bonus

Bonus schemes are designed to motivate employees by rewarding them for achieving particular targets or standards previously agreed with the employer. The idea is that this will help to recruit, motivate and retain staff and increase their understanding, involvement and commitment to the business. Some bonuses are tied to output levels; others are linked to revenue or profit. As with piecework, there can be a danger of workers concentrating on the bonus targets at the expense of other aspects of work.

Profit share

Profit share means that an agreed percentage of the profits is paid to employees, it can be in the form of cash or share options (the right to buy shares in the business at a discount). This links the performance of workers closely to the performance of the business. It is not linked to individual performance but that of the whole business, this can mean that less productive employees benefit from the hard work of others; at the same time it gives team members motivation to encourage weaker colleagues to improve. It may also be the case that external factors can influence business performance beyond the control of the employees, so their share might not reflect their efforts.

Team working usually results in improved productivity and faster problem solving.

Performance-related pay

Performance related pay is a scheme where wages or salaries are linked to performance in the workplace. There are many different schemes but generally speaking the size of the payment will depend upon how well the worker has performed and may be based on pre-agreed targets. This generally involves some form of appraisal (review of performance) conducted by senior managers, followed by appropriate targets being set for the next appraisal. Sometimes there may be disputes over how performance is measured and employees may not get on with the person doing the appraising. Some research has indicated that these schemes can demotivate some employees.

Non-financial techniques to improve employee performance

Businesses can select a combination of measures that are likely to suit their own particular people and situations. In addition to the financial incentives set out above, there are many non-financial measures that can enhance motivation. If these succeed, the motivated employee is likely to be happier and more productive and to do a better job.

The business may move away from a hierarchical structure by delayering (removing layers of management). This moves it towards more democratic leadership styles and tends to improve communication. All or most employees then assume more responsibilities and many will find this rewarding. This can improve commitment and loyalty to the business.

Various changes can work well, several possibilities are summarised below.

Delegation means handing individuals more responsibility for making decisions, this encourages initiative and increases motivation.

Consultation involves discussions with employees about working methods and practices. This creates a feeling of importance and of being valued for more than just their labour, thus increasing motivation.

Empowerment is a term used to describe ways in which employees can make independent decisions without consulting a manager, often giving more freedom than simple delegation. It increases feelings of self-worth and improves morale and motivation, as well as generating new ideas.

Team working involves organising employees into teams that share decision making and responsibility for production. This usually results in improved productivity and faster problem solving.

Flexible working is a general term for any arrangement that allows employees to have a more variable work schedule. It can give employees more control over their working lives and increase their job satisfaction.

Job enrichment means giving employees meaningful whole tasks to do, rather than boring, repetitive fragments of work. Herzberg defined it as "Giving people the opportunity to use their ability." It increases motivation.

Job rotation allows employees to change jobs, this introduces variety and reduces the time they spend repeating tedious or routine processes that can lead to boredom and carelessness.

Job enlargement means increasing the range of tasks an employee is expected to perform, often involving multi-skilling. As with job rotation, it brings variety and reduces boredom. It also brings a greater sense of responsibility and motivation.

Because people and organisations vary, there is no one magic approach which is guaranteed to improve motivation. For example, delegation and empowerment are received positively by most people but there are some who shy away from responsibility and want to be told what to do. The Hawthorne effect showed that paying attention to people generally has a positive impact. The biggest mistake can be to take motivation for granted, giving no thought to worker attitudes and preferences.

Chapter 18

Leadership

Leadership

Leadership is one of the key skills involved in running a successful business. It has been defined as the art of motivating and organising a group of people to achieve a common goal. The more effectively this can be done, the more successful the business will be.

The distinction between management and leadership

The main distinction is that leaders have people who follow them while managers have people who work for them.

In years gone by leadership and management were seen as being different and separate. The factory foreman or manager was there to make sure that the workers knew what to do and that it got done. They had no connection with the strategy of the business or particular interest in the worker as a person with a personality. Their job was not to inspire but to be efficient.

In today's world a successful entrepreneur needs to be both a strong leader and a manager. Leadership is about getting people to understand and believe in your vision and to work with you to achieve your goals, this means encouraging your staff to develop their full potential and to inspire their work. At the same time the business needs to be organised and efficient. Even the most exciting and inspiring leaders have to worry about managing the nuts and bolts of the operation.

Richard Branson, with the casual image, the balloons, the spaceships and all the razzamatazz is one of our best known business leaders and is indelibly associated with the Virgin brand, yet he is also a shrewd and capable manager and leader. One of the reasons for his apparent thirst for publicity is that this reinforces Virgin's vision to his staff as well as to customers.

Management without leadership is possible, and is perhaps functional but uninspiring. Leadership adds vision and direction, but leadership not underpinned by management could be chaotic. It is possible for good leaders to work with good managers, but ideally a strong leader should have both skills.

Main leadership styles

People bring their own personal qualities to the task of leadership but there are four main types of leadership style:

Autocratic

Autocratic managers keep power in their own hands and make all the important decisions. Sometimes they try to make all the minor decisions too. They give orders without consulting anyone else. This is a top-down, one-way system of communication that can often be described as dictatorial. Autocratic managers like to control the situation they are in. Decision making is quick because there is no consultation. However, this type of management style can decrease motivation and increase staff turnover because staff may not feel valued if their views are never sought.

Paternalistic

Paternalistic leaders, as the name implies, act as a father might towards their family. They think they know best and although there is some consideration, consultation and involvement, it is ultimately the leader who takes responsibility and decides what happens. Many paternalistic leaders are confident that their decisions will be the best for the business. Communication is mostly top-down but with some two-way dialogue. Subordinates feel that they are valued to an extent, but there is no doubt about who is in control. Think David Brent from The Office!

Democratic

Democratic leaders listen to other people's ideas and opinions and take them into account before reaching a decision. There is a two-way system of communication; tasks and minor decisions are likely to be delegated, giving employees responsibility to complete the task given to them (also known as empower-ment). As employees are involved in decision making, they feel a sense of belonging and ownership so motivation is likely to be high. Although popular in business today, a democratic management style can slow decision making down because staff need to be consulted, this can be too slow and unwieldy in some dynamic markets. Some leaders who describe themselves as democratic are seen by others as reluctant to let go of ultimate power so more paternalistic.

Laissez-faire

A laissez faire leader will set the initial agenda, then stand back, giving staff maximum freedom to complete their tasks as they see fit. This does not mean that the leader is inactive, rather that they are there to answer questions, supply information and give advice if needed. The benefit of a laissez faire management style is that staff can thrive on personal responsibility for tasks, leading to improved motivation and staff confidence. This sort of style may be particularly suited to creative industries where staff can come up with imaginative products and solutions when they are freed from the shackles of conventional management. In a fast changing environment, laissez-faire allows people to make instant decisions. However, the danger is that a laissez-faire leader who does not provide adequate guidance may have staff who feel lost and who might not reach their objectives or meet deadlines.

Leadership styles summary

Style	Key features
Autocratic	The boss alone makes decisions.
Paternalistic	The boss cares about others' views but still decides.
Democratic	Consultation, delegation and shared decisions.
Laissez-faire	Maximum freedom for individuals to shape their work.

Leadership styles in action

In the past, most leadership styles in manufacturing businesses would have been autocratic. Think, for example, of the attitudes involved in Taylor's scientific management. In the second half of the 20th century, Japanese industrialists showed how teamwork could be organised to bring high standards of quality and reliability. (This is sometimes called The Japanese Way.) Discussion about how the best outcome might be achieved was encouraged and ideas from anywhere in the organisation were taken seriously. In the light of this experience, there has been a trend towards more democratic leadership styles.

Leadership styles depend heavily on the personality and confidence of the entrepreneur or the manager. But they also depend on the nature of the business and the traditions within the industry. Successful sole traders whose businesses expand into large organisations often struggle to 'let go of the reins' since the business was built on their energy and ideas. People who move straight into management roles after graduating with relevant degrees come from very different backgrounds. However, whatever they have learned about leadership can only be applied if their personality is appropriate.

In reality, leaders will often exhibit some or all of the leadership styles at different times and in different contexts. In a crisis, for example, clear direction might be more important than allowing everyone to pull in different directions. Think of it as a Venn diagram. The mix of styles adopted by a leader/manager will vary according to the situation. The best leaders will understand their colleagues and know how best to treat them. Good leaders know which style to use or adapt at any given time to get the best from their staff and the best result for the business.

Think!

Consider organisations you are involved with, perhaps in a part-time job, where you study or even in your household.

What leadership styles do you see? What evidence leads you to your view on this?

Can you (tactfully) find out whether the leaders share your view on their styles?

Exam style question

Leadership styles and motivation

Albert J Dunlap took over as Chief Executive Officer of The Sunbeam Corporation in 1996. In his 20 month spell as CEO he was renowned for his ruthlessness. He fired 11,000 people or 40 percent of the workforce. While this move improved profitability and raised share prices, the loss of talent meant that the company faced erosion of value, leading to long-term decline.

Berkshire Hathaway is the holding company of Warren Buffet the world famous financier. In one of its recent annual reports he wrote "We tend to let our many subsidiaries operate on their own, without our supervising and monitoring them to any degree."

Ingvar Kamprad is the founder of IKEA, the world's biggest retailer of home furnishing. Its values are very much family based and Kamprad treats his employees as if they are part of the family. Although Kamprad listens to his employees he is very much the boss.

Between 1991 and 2012 Ratan Tata was head of the Tata Group, the giant and hugely successful Indian multinational company. He encouraged his managers to be innovative and share all their ideas, consulting actively with them and encouraging team-working. They were well informed about future strategy and engaged in the decision making process.

Questions

1. What is meant by leadership? *(2 marks)*

2. What is meant by motivation? *(2 marks)*

3. Explain the likely impact of Albert Dunlap's leadership on worker motivation at The Sunbeam Corporation. *(4 marks)*

4. Explain two advantages of Ratan Tata's leadership style. *(4 marks)*

5. Examine strengths and weaknesses of Ingvar Kamprad's leadership style at Ikea. *(8 marks)*

6. Assess the suggestion that good leadership strengthens worker motivation, making some reference to examples from the extract above. *(10 marks)*

Chapter 19

Role of an entrepreneur

An entrepreneur can be briefly defined as someone who organises a business venture and is responsible for the risks involved. The entrepreneur will decide what will be produced and how it will be created, organise the finance to cover start-up costs and decide the price at which to market output. Once the business is up and running, the entrepreneur will continue to take responsibility for its ongoing success.

Entrepreneurs come in all shapes and sizes; some are household names such as Philip Green, Anita Roddick, Victoria Beckham, Alan Sugar and Richard Branson. For every public face like these, there are many other equally successful entrepreneurs who are almost anonymous. Ayman Asfari runs oil services group Petrofac, a FTSE 100 business that manages oil rigs from Aberdeen, via the UAE, to India, as well as designing drilling and refinery equipment. Back in the 90's Denise Coates noticed the growing popularity of online gambling and in 2000 launched Bet365; by 2014 this hugely successful business had profits of £213.8m on £1.37bn of sales.

Most entrepreneurs are not high profile or as well known, in fact the great majority run small businesses. The plumber who comes to mend your leaking pipe is just as much an entrepreneur as Alan Sugar.

> **Entrepreneurs** are people who bring factors of production together to create a desirable product.

Creating and setting up a business

Businesses are created when an entrepreneur combines resources in order to produce either a product or a service. Resources consist of labour (the human input), raw materials and capital. Capital can mean the money used to start a business in everyday language, to an economist it means anything that is used repeatedly to produce something else. This includes many things such as premises, machinery, computers, office equipment and vehicles. A budding entrepreneur will need to have not just a business idea but the ability to obtain the necessary resources and to organise transforming the starting idea to reality.

In 2014, a record breaking 581,173 businesses were registered with Companies House, an increase on previous years with 526,447 and 484,224 recorded in 2013 and 2012 respectively. This gives some idea of the scale of entrepreneurship in the UK. These businesses will range from the high-tech and cutting edge part of the spectrum to the more everyday electricians, cake shops and cafes. Much of the increase can be explained by the recovering UK economy and the benefits of digital technology. Of course not all these businesses will succeed, in 2014 the number of firms dropping out of the Companies House register was 238,000.

Running and expanding/developing a business

Creating a business is only the start of it; the statistics above suggest that for every two businesses created one will fail. For many entrepreneurs, starting a business is relatively straightforward; the tricky bit is surviving and then expanding. The abilities needed to launch a business are not the same as those needed to help it grow. In the early days the entrepreneur will need to adopt a 'hands-on' approach, dealing with all aspects of the business and sorting problems out as they arise. Expansion will mean bringing in extra staff with different areas of expertise and ability. As the business grows the entrepreneur needs to be able to stand back a little and delegate, to trust others and give up day-to-day control of every detail, otherwise excessive interference could smother initiative and motivation. For many successful entrepreneurs, learning to listen to, and take, advice is one of the hardest challenges they face.

Complacency can be a major threat to a growing business. An entrepreneur who assumes that success will automatically continue following a successful launch is likely to be mistaken. Successful expansion requires the entrepreneur to re-visit and update the business plan (see Theme 2). Market research must be ongoing to keep up with market trends; planning ahead is crucial and careful financial management is needed – particularly with cash flow. For a growing business this is important, cash constraints can be the biggest factor limiting growth and overtrading (expanding too quickly without the necessary finance) can cause the business to fail.

Example

Apple's philosophy is all about repeatedly designing products that work really well, look good and appeal to customers. The company has excelled in this and as a result has been able to charge very high prices without losing market share. By the end of 2017 record profits were being made. Clearly, even if high quality design is an important business objective for Apple, profit maximisation is at least equally important. If it were not so, their prices might be lower.

Innovation within a business (intrapreneurship)

Gifford Pinchot wrote in 1984 that intrapreneurs are *"…dreamers who do. Those who take hands-on responsibility for creating innovation of any kind, within a business."* In 1985 Steve Jobs said *"The Macintosh team was what is commonly known as Intrapreneurship."* Many multinationals and other large businesses rely on a stream of intrapreneurial ideas to build and protect their positions in markets.

Intrapreneurship focuses on those employees within a business that have many of the attributes of entrepreneurs. An intrapreneur is someone within a business that takes risks in an effort to solve a given problem. They possess entrepreneurial skills and use them within a company, instead of using them to launch a new business.

Whilst the entrepreneur has an overall vision of the company as a whole and where it is headed in the long run, the intrapreneur will usually focus on a specific part of the business, either to find a way round an existing problem or to be creative in improving overall productivity and to increase the capacity of the business.

Sir Richard Branson stated that Virgin could never have grown into the group of more than 200 companies it is now, were it not for a steady stream of intrapreneurs who looked for and developed opportunities. Ken Kutaragi, a Sony Employee, spent hours adapting his daughter's Nintendo to make it more powerful and user friendly. Despite initial scepticism from the Sony board his work led to the development of one of Sony's most successful products, the Playstation.

Facebook holds 'hackathons', where engineers collaborate on software projects outside of their normal day job. Some ideas have turned into real features for the site including the famous 'like' button. Google also encourages its employees to pursue personal projects. Paul Buchheit started on his project in 2001 this eventually became Gmail, which was launched in 2004.

These are famous examples that have had a dramatic impact on the businesses concerned, but intrapreneurship takes place in all sorts of businesses and in all sorts of ways. Good entrepreneurs know the value of intrapreneurship and the benefits of encouraging it.

> **Intrapreneurs** are people who bring innovation to existing businesses rather than to business start-ups. They can improve products, processes or productivity.

Barriers to entrepreneurship

There are many reasons why the road to entrepreneurship is difficult for most people. Even if you have a worthwhile idea on paper, there are still many obstacles that can prevent you from succeeding. It is entrepreneurs that will create the wealth and economic growth in the UK economy, the government knows this and is trying to break down some of the barriers by a range of initiatives including the New Enterprise Allowance Scheme (NEAS) which aims to provide assistance for those making the transition from unemployment to self-employment.

There are several broad areas of difficulty that act as barriers to entrepreneurship. There appears to be a lack of cultural understanding and appreciation of entrepreneurship that runs right through the public sector and society. The Global Entrepreneurship and Development Index places the UK in the bottom quarter globally for the number of people who perceive entrepreneurship to be a good career choice. In other cultures, such as the USA, far more people tend to be entrepreneurial. Much more needs to be done in schools, training centres and universities to develop the importance of entrepreneurship.

Think!

Do you know any entrepreneurs?

If so, do they have special qualities?

What might hold you back from becoming an entrepreneur, if anything?

Certain groups in society still find it harder than it should be to become entrepreneurs. The Department for Business, Innovation and Skills has found that only 29% of entrepreneurs are women. If the start-up rate for women equalled that of men, 150,000 additional businesses would be created each year. Other groups facing similar difficulties include the unemployed, the disabled and ex-members of the armed forces. These difficulties may be caused by a range of factors including discrimination, lack of opportunity, bureaucracy and red tape.

The biggest practical barrier to entrepreneurship is undoubtedly access to finance. This has always been a problem, but has become much worse since the financial crisis as banks have become much more reluctant to lend. Banks increasingly tend not to lend to businesses without suitable security; this makes life difficult for small businesses and specifically deters business start-ups.

Anticipating risk and uncertainty in the business environment

"Businesses don't plan to fail – they fail to plan" – old business saying.

Facing and dealing with risk is part of the job description for any entrepreneur. Business survival and expansion requires taking risks. Successful businesses manage risk well, while those that do not may suffer. Risk can be measured and therefore minimised if the entrepreneur has knowledge. In business, good knowledge is a key to success; knowing as much as possible about the market, the consumers, the competition and the economy can help to reduce both risk and, to an extent, uncertainty.

Successful entrepreneurs take calculated risks and try to reduce the odds against them. If a business is launching a new product, then the more the business knows about the new market the more it can adapt and accurately target that market to reduce the risk of failure. Successful businesses have to be flexible and able to adapt rapidly; implementing change when uncertainty hits. Speed can be critical in this and therefore a flexible management and workforce is crucial.

Financial control and financial planning are important areas of risk reduction; there are many useful techniques and measures that can be used to help the managers make informed decisions. A range of these will appear in subsequent parts of this course.

Contingency planning means having a plan in readiness in case of a crisis or an unwanted event. It is not just about major disasters like a terrorist attack. It's also about preparing for events on a smaller scale such as the loss of data, people, customers or suppliers, and other unknowns. Thinking about potential problems in advance helps the business to recover faster when something has gone wrong. If problems do occur, then the business is ready and can save time and possibly expense. Contingency plans need to be developed and also continuously reviewed and updated.

A Dragon speaks...

"50% of all small businesses fail in the first couple of years. It's a damning statistic but it's true. They haven't done the research, they don't know where to go for the right funding... it's rarely one thing. The reason people fail is because they don't do their homework. You wouldn't sit an exam without doing any preparation and a business is no different. It's about knowing more than the next guy or girl and performing better, and the only way you can do that is through knowledge. It's basic stuff but we don't do it."

Theo Paphitis

Theo Paphitis, entrepreneur and former star of Dragons' Den on why so many would-be entrepreneurs fail to succeed.

To what extent do you think Theo Paphitis is right?

Explain why the government might want to encourage entrepreneurship

What could the government do to help prevent so many small businesses failing?

Chapter 20

Entrepreneurial motives and characteristics

Ecotricity

Ecotricity describes its mission as "to change the way electricity is made and used in Britain." Dale Vince, the founder, has structured the business to pay no dividends to shareholders but to reinvest profits in additional green energy production capacity. His declared ambition is to help make Britain "a place in which we all live more sustainable lives and where ethical business is the norm – pursuing outcomes other than profit." How and what a business does will have an impact on many people.

Discussion point

Do you consider Dale Vince's motivation unusual?

Some people say that entrepreneurs are born not made, that it just comes naturally to some people. There are of course, plenty of examples of entrepreneurs who have all the skills needed to succeed, despite little in the way of formal education or training. Philip Green left school at 15, Richard Branson, James Caan and Alan Sugar at 16, yet they have all been immensely successful. They seem to have an instinctive grasp of entrepreneurial skills.

On the other hand, there are many formal academic qualifications in business related subjects, including degrees in business start-ups. There are many highly qualified entrepreneurs with specialist qualifications; many have taken MBAs (Master of Business Administration). The government provides a range of services to support the would-be entrepreneur, including Business Link and the Department of Business, Innovation and Skills.

The National Enterprise Academy, backed by Peter Jones from Dragons Den, is designed to prepare young people for an entrepreneurial career. However, whether an entrepreneur is born or made they tend to share common characteristics and skills

Characteristics and skills required

Hard work – Without hard work an entrepreneur is unlikely to succeed. This usually means more than the usual 9 to 5 hours, especially in the early days of a business. Committed entrepreneurs will constantly be thinking about the business and working to improve it.

Motivation – An entrepreneur needs to be well motivated, with a strong desire to succeed. There will inevitably be setbacks and problems to solve. Without strong motivation to overcome these, the business may fail.

Risk-taking – An entrepreneur must be prepared to take risks. Business entails having the foresight to take calculated risks at the right time, in order to be successful. Would-be entrepreneurs who are too cautious are likely to be left behind. Equally, those who are not alert to the inevitable risks may try to do too much too soon and then find they are losing money and their business is in trouble.

Initiative – Entrepreneurs do not need to be told what to do. They see and seize upon opportunities to advance the business, using their experience, initiative and perhaps gut instincts.

Creativity – Entrepreneurs need to be able to come up with good ideas or a fresh way of looking at things, in order to create and maintain a competitive advantage.

Resilience – Life as an entrepreneur will not be easy or straightforward. Setbacks and failures are commonplace and the entrepreneur has to accept the setbacks, learn from the mistakes and carry on. Self-confidence can help entrepreneurs to survive.

Perseverance/commitment – Without 100% commitment a business is unlikely to succeed. There will be a constant series of problems to solve. Markets are dynamic and need constant monitoring.

Understanding the market – Good entrepreneurs know their market well. This means having an understanding of their customers' needs and wants, their rivals' likely plans and the direction and future of the market as a whole. Successful entrepreneurs can cope with the competition from rival businesses.

Reasons why people set up businesses

For many people the answer may be obvious – they will say it is all about making profits and getting rich. This may be true for some entrepreneurs but not for all. People like Philip Green, Richard Branson or Rupert Murdoch have long since passed the getting rich stage; they could have retired to a life of luxury long ago. Something else is keeping them going.

On a much smaller scale, the newly self-employed plumber or artist is probably not dreaming of their first million. They are more likely to be looking forward to working independently, or the satisfaction of following their artistic leanings. This does not mean that profit is unimportant, rather that there are many other things that can motivate entrepreneurs.

There are always some shrinking and failing businesses in a dynamic economy. This entails some people becoming unemployed. When new jobs are hard to find, as in a recession, starting a small business can be the best option available to someone desperate to earn a living. Record numbers of people entered self-employment and started small businesses during and after the last recession.

Financial motives: profit maximisation and profit satisficing

Many people run a business primarily to make money, to improve their lifestyle and secure a good standard of living for themselves and their families. Profit – the difference between sales revenue and costs – will reward successful entrepreneurs for both the hard work and the risks they have had to live with. Some entrepreneurs will aim to make as much money as possible – profit maximisation.

It may be more accurate to talk about short and long term profit maximisation. With short-term profit maximisation there is a danger that the pursuit of short-term profits can ignore longer term strategic interests. If a business devotes all of its resources to whichever product is currently in high demand and yielding high profits, it may fail to invest and develop new products This means missing out on future opportunities. Long-term profit maximisation would avoid this pitfall and use the business' resources to maximum effect, pursuing both short and long run profitability.

Not all entrepreneurs are motivated solely by the size of the profits they make. For many, a level of profits that enables them to continue in business and have a reasonable material standard of living may be enough. If they are motivated by other factors such as being independent and the lifestyle that their business brings, they may not be interested in taking on the additional risk and effort involved to maximise profits. This is called profit satisficing.

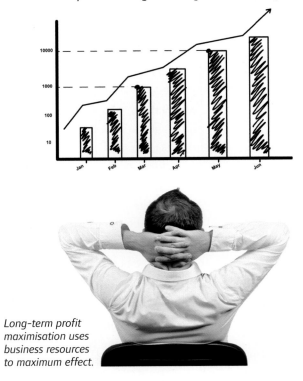

Long-term profit maximisation uses business resources to maximum effect.

Satisficing is a term first used by Herbert Simon in 1957, and means attempting to take into account a number of different and competing objectives, without attempting to 'maximise' any single one. It entails not maximising profit because other considerations also have an influence on behaviour. You have probably come across students who satisfice in their academic work, balancing attainment against other personal or social objectives.

'Impact Investment' is a term which has attracted increased attention in the USA. It centres on providing a good or service that has a positive social impact whilst also generating some financial return. At a minimum, this entails creating wealth rather than simply transferring income from others to the entrepreneur. People often go well beyond this minimum to target specific social objectives alongside earning an income. However, there are those who argue that simply making money from a business one is good at, then donating generously to worthy causes, is a very effective way of helping others.

> **Profit maximising** means aiming to make as much profit as possible, pursuing this objective regardless of other considerations.
>
> **Profit satisficing** means having other objectives which influence decision making, accepting less than maximum profits in order to combine 'enough' income with other priorities.

Non-financial motives

Social, Ethical and Green considerations – an increasing number of entrepreneurs want to do the 'right' thing and look beyond their own selfish interests. Their businesses are primarily centred on providing ethical and/or environmentally friendly products. For example, One Water uses its profits to improve supplies of clean water by providing water pumps in African villages.

> A **social entrepreneur** is someone who uses their business to achieve benefits for society.

The main aim of social entrepreneurship is to further social and environmental goals. Duncan Goose, who created One Water, would come under this heading. So would Muhammad Yunus, who won the Nobel Peace Prize in 2006 for his founding of the Grameen Bank, which provides credit and banking services to the rural poor in Bangladesh.

Employee welfare – another 'social' motivation can be to provide work and incomes for a group of people. One person or a group set out to create a business which meets the needs of a number of people. It is quite common for this type of business to be organised as a cooperative. Sometimes, as in the case of the John Lewis Partnership, large businesses are based on employee ownership and welfare.

Example

Suma is a vegetarian wholefoods wholesaler based in Leeds, specialising in healthy, natural, organic and Fairtrade foods. From modest beginnings 40 years ago, the organisation has moved to bigger premises several times to allow expansion. It now employs around 150 people and has sales revenue of more than £34 million per year. The business was well placed to gain from growing interest in healthy eating. Its approach to business has also proved very successful.

Suma is an equal opportunity, fully democratic workers' cooperative. All the members/employees have the same hourly rate of pay. Members are multi-skilled, bringing flexibility to the business and variety to each person's work. General meetings decide policy and direction. An elected management committee oversees the fulfilment of plans. An emphasis on ethical behaviour and working for sustainability has always been important to Suma.

Additional objectives for some entrepreneurs can include:

Self-actualisation – sometimes being able to achieve a dream or an ambition, however modest, is reward enough for taking on the role and risks of being an entrepreneur.

Customer satisfaction – some entrepreneurs derive pleasure from operating a business which meets people's needs, often as one element in a satisficing mix of objectives.

Creativity – for some entrepreneurs the need to produce or build something is the main motive whether it is an artist or potter, an architect or a builder. The satisfaction of seeing their vision become real is the driving motive.

Satisfaction of making things happen – the ability to get things moving, to create and achieve deals that lead to more business. This is often the main driving force behind successful entrepreneurs who are not necessarily motivated by money.

Independence – being your own boss is a strong motivating factor for many people, knowing that their decisions and not someone else's will determine the success of the business. The absence of a superior giving orders is a real attraction for independent-minded people who do not relish a 9-5 existence.

Home working – being able to work from home gives many entrepreneurs the chance to balance the needs of a home life and family with developing a business idea. Time and money are saved by not commuting, and in the early stages there is no need to take on the cost of premises if the home environment is suitable.

People are complicated and can have many alternative motives and combinations of motives. It is not unusual for events to develop in ways which change people's thinking, actions or even their motivations. Some of the people who become self-employed might happily switch back to employment as and when an opportunity arises. Some will find contentment in running their small business. A few will find their businesses growing into large organisations and then exploit the opportunity to grow rich or to pursue more ambitious objectives than they once thought possible.

The macaron queen of India

Pooja Dhingra was studying law at university in Mumbai, when she decided that she wanted to quit and to do something more creative. In 2008 she changed course and went to Paris to be a pastry chef, once there she tasted her first macaron (the English equivalent is macaroon) and decided that when she returned to Mumbai she would open her own macaron store, the first of its kind in India.

Returning to Mumbai she set to work in her parents' kitchen at developing her own macaron recipe. The weather in Mumbai is substantially hotter and more humid than Paris and she struggled for six months with the heat and humidity which made it difficult to make the delicate cakes. Other problems included the red tape and bureaucracy; she also found it difficult to overcome male prejudice when it came to being taken seriously in business deals.

After more than 60 different recipes she finally found one that worked and secured the premises for a small commercial kitchen in 2010. The first shop followed and she now employs 40 people and has three shops.

To build up sales in a city where very few people knew what a macaron was, Pooja gave away free samples. She also started running classes on how to make macarons and other cakes, which gave the business a further promotional boost.

She wants other young women, both in India and overseas, to start their own companies. "Once you are passionate about what you want to do you will achieve it," she says. "The hours will be long and challenges will appear, but if you are passionate enough you will succeed."

What difficulties did Pooja have to overcome?

What entrepreneurial characteristics has she shown? Explain your answers.

What do you think motivates Pooja?

Chapter 21

Business objectives

Different objectives

One Vision Housing is an award winning housing provider, with 13,000 homes for rent in Merseyside, primarily across the borough of Sefton. *"We are committed to creating sustainable neighbourhoods; thriving, well run, active, inclusive and most importantly, safe places to live. Places that people are proud of and want to live in."* (quote from their website)

Aldi opened its first store in 1913, since then it has established itself in international markets including Germany, Australia, the UK and the USA. What distinguishes Aldi from its competitors is its competitive pricing strategy; in some cases Aldi's products are 30% cheaper than those offered by its competitors. Aldi can do this because the business operates so efficiently.

Marks and Spencer launched their Plan A in 2007. This is how their website describes it today. *"Plan A is our way to help protect the planet – by sourcing responsibly, reducing waste and helping communities. We launched Plan A in January 2007, setting out 100 commitments to achieve in 5 years. We've now introduced Plan A 2020 which consists of 100 new, revised and existing commitments, with the ultimate goal of becoming the world's most sustainable major retailer."*

In early 2018, Apple announced that it had made $88.3bn in revenue during the final quarter of 2017, with a profit of $20bn, or $3.89 per share. Both were records. Apple's consistently large share of industry profits is particularly notable because the company accounts for a relatively small portion of global sales.

Acer, the Taiwanese electronics and computer giant, provides a range of benefits for its employees in Taiwan. These include organised activities for employees and their families such as 2-3 day tours, family days and arts appreciation activities. They also provide subsidies and funds for a variety of social activities. The factories have relaxation areas including massage chairs, electronic games facilities, exercise facilities, a lounge and cafés. They also give employees vouchers for the three major festivals (Chinese New Year, Dragon Boat Festival, and Mid-Autumn Festival) as well as birthdays, along with scholarships and cash subsidies for weddings and funerals.

What do you think are the main objectives of these five businesses? (there may be more than one). Explain your answers.

Why are they pursuing these objectives?

What might cause them to change?

All businesses have objectives; these are goals that the business wants to achieve over a period of time. The motivation of the entrepreneur or other owners will play a major part in shaping business objectives. These objectives may change depending on the situation of the business. For example, a new business may have the simple objective of surviving for the first two years. Once established the objective may change to one of growth or profit maximisation.

Business objectives are not mutually exclusive, they often go hand in hand and reinforce one another, a desire to maximise profits can also mean trying to achieve cost efficiency and an increase in market share.

Business objectives are determined by a range of factors, for example small businesses may be content with profit satisfising or survival, larger businesses may want to maximise growth and market share. Short-term objectives may differ from long-term ones. Objectives are also shaped by the influence of stakeholders within the organisation; employees may want to maximise their welfare, managers may want to pursue sales targets to achieve bonuses and shareholders may exert pressure to fulfil profit or/and environmental and social objectives.

Survival

All businesses are likely to consider survival to be their main objective at various times. To state the obvious, unless a business survives it cannot fulfil any other objectives and there will be times when survival is all that matters. It is not just new businesses that need to survive, changing market and economic conditions can threaten even the most famous of names. There are three main circumstances that will cause a business to prioritise survival.

In the early stages of development businesses are vulnerable for many reasons, they may lack resources and experience; sales can be unpredictable as customers have yet to recognise the brand or to develop loyalty and competition can be fierce for a new business. All of which means that the business is likely to have survival as its main objective until it can grow and become established.

Difficult trading conditions such as those experienced in the recent recession can alter a business' objectives. Many failed to survive the initial financial crisis, such as Lehman Brothers, the fourth-largest investment bank in the US which declared bankruptcy in 2008. In the UK businesses such as Comet limped on until 2012 before closing. Others survived but only just, HMV suffered from the downturn in the economy and competition from the digital sector. At the time of writing high street names such as Thornton's and Tesco are struggling as trading conditions change.

Businesses can sometimes become the targets of a takeover bid. When this happens the survival of the business in its existing shape becomes paramount. Directors and managers may try to persuade shareholders not to sell shares to the rival company. Cadbury tried in vain to resist being taken over by Kraft Foods. Again, at the time of writing Mylan, a multinational pharmaceutical company with head offices in Hertfordshire is resisting a hostile takeover bid from Teva, an Israeli company.

In the long term though, survival is unlikely to be the main or longest lasting objective, owners will switch to other objectives once danger is past.

Profit maximisation

Profit maximisation occurs when the difference between total revenue and total costs is at its greatest. Many assume this to be the most important objective for a business. Shareholders have invested money into the business and expect to be rewarded in the form of dividends and increased share values. At the same time as looking after its shareholders with dividends, the business has to generate enough profit to help finance investment for future growth.

Sales maximisation is not the same as profit maximisation as it is likely to reduce profit as a result of dropping prices.

Profit maximisation can be a destructive and short term objective if care is not taken. Profits could be increased by using cheaper and poorer quality inputs, wages could be cut, customer service reduced and environmental rules may be ignored and so on. All of these measures may lead to profit maximisation in the short-run but create long-term problems for the business.

All businesses need to make a profit but whether it is maximised will vary according to the aims of the business. Maximising profits does mean other objectives are ignored or given less priority and this may not be in line with the wishes of other stakeholders who may object. In reality profit maximising businesses will usually have other objectives running alongside.

Other objectives

Sales maximisation is not the same as profit maximisation. In fact maximising sales is likely to reduce profits, particularly as increasing sales are likely to depend on price reductions. A business that sets out to maximise sales is likely to do so for several reasons.

A Not for Profit Organisation (NPO) may do this to reach as many people as possible to further their work or cause, examples include housing trusts, cooperatives, trade unions, credit unions, industry associations and sports clubs, many have charitable status.

More conventional businesses may try to maximise sales to build up their customer base and market share at the expense of their rivals. Increased market share can lead to increased market power, less risk and more profits in the long run when the now bigger business has more control over the market.

A business may find itself with excess stock and/or the need to improve cash flow, in which case, selling the maximum number of products may well be the most important objective. It may even be the case that managers are awarded bonuses if they meet ever higher sales targets, which encourages them to focus on sales maximisation.

Market share gives a clear idea of progress and is a good measure of business performance compared to rivals. To aim to increase market share from 15% to 25% sets a clear objective. New entrants might have a market share target. Of course, market share statistics have to be interpreted with care. The rate of change in the overall market has to be taken into account as well.

Like sales maximisation, market share can be a short term objective. A big enough share brings market power which might help in achieving long term objectives. However, for some businesses it is a permanent priority. Stability and security as an established supplier in the market can be more important than profit, though these objectives can be linked. Leading business owners in a community may value their position as the leading local provider of their product or service.

Cost efficiency concentrates on the relationship between inputs and corresponding outputs, if this enables a business to undercut the costs and prices of rivals it can lead to a competitive advantage. Businesses that focus on cost efficiency may well be using this as a way of reaching other objectives such as increasing market share or maximising profits. Cost efficiency is particularly important when revenue is static or falling and will also contribute to profitability. Through being efficient and cutting costs a business can then invest profits back into the business. This can then be used to further meet its other business objectives.

Operating efficiently with minimum waste and the lowest possible unit costs (cost efficiency) can become a source of pride and satisfaction as well as profit. This can become an objective in itself.

Example
Xerox research suggested that 40% of office paper is discarded within a day of being printed; paperless systems cut costs, waste and resource use. A business which goes paperless for internal communications might thereby gain in cost efficiency – as long as communications were still effective.

Employee welfare includes anything that is done for the comfort and wellbeing of the employees and is provided over and above wages. It will help to improve the morale and motivation of the employees which may benefit the business in the form of increased productivity, lower staff turnover and therefore reduced recruitment and training costs. For cooperatives this can be a very important objective. Again, this will contribute to other business objectives.

Customer satisfaction might be more accurately referred to as customer pressure. For businesses that rely on consumers for sales then satisfying consumer wants has obvious importance, particularly where repeat sales are involved. This may take the form of addressing the need for environmentally sustainable and responsible products, adopting an ethical stance, cutting down on waste and providing a friendly and helpful service. In a competitive market this can help to differentiate a company's products and may allow a premium price to be charged to more discerning customers. Ignoring customer wants can lead to a worsening reputation and even consumer action and boycotts.

Social objectives are when the business focusses on achieving a goal that benefits the community, the environment or sectors of society not directly related to the business. Such objectives are often found in social enterprises (see next section) which may, for example, employ ex-prisoners or disabled people, and also in more conventional businesses with Corporate Social Responsibility (CSR) programmes. These may centre on Fairtrade, an ethical sourcing policy or ethical treatment of workers.

"There is one and only one social responsibility of business – to use its resources and engage in activities designed to increase its profits so long as it stays within the rules of the game, which is to say, engages in open and free competition without deception or fraud." – *Milton Friedman*

"Profit is not the purpose of business and the concept of profit maximisation is not only meaningless, but dangerous." – *Peter F. Drucker*

TerraCycle

TerraCycle is a recycling and upcycling business which aims to find waste and turn it into something useful, for a profit. Founder Tom Szaky moved from Hungary to Canada and was struck by the mountains of material thrown out in rich communities. TerraCycle's first activity was collecting organic waste and feeding it to worms, then selling the resulting fertiliser in recycled plastic bottles, as plant food.

Not all activities have been profitable. A bag called the 'reTote', made from used plastic bags, was sold to a distributor for a few dollars each though the costs were more than $10 per unit. Despite this, the company has grown in 13 years, to have revenue of $20m p.a. and 115 employees. It operates in several countries.

Much of the collection of waste materials is now done by volunteers organised in 'brigades'. The volunteers get nothing tangible for themselves but are rewarded by donations to charity and 'a good feeling'. TerraCycle make few products themselves. They collect the waste and design products and processes. Others are then licensed to make, market and sell the products. An unnamed British company is in talks to buy 20% of the business for around $20m.

What do you see as the objectives of Terracycle?

What are the likely objectives of the brigades of volunteers?

Chapter 22

Forms of business

Ben Cohen and Jerry Greenfield became friends at high school. Shared interests included a love of good food and a social conscience. After a correspondence course in ice-cream making, they invested $12,000 and opened their first Ben & Jerry's ice-cream shop in 1978.

The Business became a company as Ben & Jerry's Homemade Holdings Incorporated. In 1985 they opened the Ben & Jerry foundation to fund community orientated projects. In 2000 Ben & Jerry's became a subsidiary of Unilever, the multinational. However, it retains a commitment to the original partners' vision.

Discussion points

What advantages might Ben & Jerry have gained from working together?

What are the benefits to the business of becoming part of a multinational company?

All businesses need a legal structure and there are advantages and disadvantages to each type. Which one a business chooses to become will depend upon its particular situation and needs. The most common types are sole trader, partnership, private limited company and public limited company. Different business structures have pros and cons that are often closely connected to their financial needs. Business start-ups usually need to be as uncomplicated as possible because they will usually be small. If the risks are low, operating as a sole trader or a partnership is the simplest of all.

Liability means responsibility for the financial debts of the business.

Sole traders and **partnerships** have **unlimited liability** which means that the owners have a legal duty for all debts and can have all of their personal possessions seized to pay the debts.

Limited companies are legal entities and their **liability is limited** to the business itself and not the owners/shareholders. The company may lose its assets but the personal wealth of the owners is protected.

Sole trader, partnership and private limited company

A **sole trade**r is an individual who runs his or her own business. They are self-employed and usually run small businesses e.g. plumbers, builders, hairdressers. A sole trader has full responsibility for the running of the business, is in full control, makes all the decisions and keeps all of the profits. Setting up the business is easy and all accounts are confidential. The disadvantages are that there is no-one to share the work or responsibility, it can be difficult to take holidays or sick leave and there can be high levels of risk if the business venture fails (unlimited liability).

Limited liability is a very important factor for most people setting up businesses. Without it, many people would feel unable to go into business on their own because the risks to their families would be too great to contemplate. A hairdresser who starts a business as a sole trader, with £5,000, and eventually goes bankrupt owing £75,000, will personally have to pay back all the debts and may have to sell personal possessions such as a house to do so. If it was a limited company, the hairdresser would only lose their original £5,000 share capital.

A **partnership** shares many of the same characteristics as the sole trader except that there is more than one owner involved. Partners are jointly responsible for the running of the business and a partnership consists of two or more people who start a business together; common examples include solicitors, accountants and dentists. Partners follow the rules laid down in a partnership agreement and are said to be 'jointly and severally' liable for the business. This means that if problems occur each partner can be held responsible for all the debts of the business if the other partner(s) have no assets. Despite this disadvantage, a partnership can have many advantages over a sole trader. A partner may bring more start-up capital and have extra skills/abilities useful to the business. The workload and responsibility can be shared and make it easier to take holidays or sick leave, problems can be discussed and it may be easier to come up with solutions. On the other hand partners can fall out and the business still has unlimited liability.

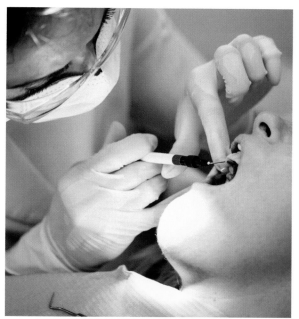

Dentists are a common example of partnerships.

To become a **Limited company** a business has to go through a legal process called incorporation. All limited companies must be registered ('incorporated') with Companies House. This is a simple process but there are strict requirements. The company must have a name, an address, at least one director and one shareholder, and the agreement of all initial shareholders to create the company – detailed in a 'memorandum of association'. Information on the company's shares and the rights attached to them are recorded in a 'statement of capital'. Written rules about how a company is run – known as 'articles of association' – are also required.

Once the company is registered a 'Certificate of Incorporation' is issued. This confirms that the company legally exists and shows the company number and date of formation. Any directors must submit an annual Self-Assessment tax return, and the company must submit annual accounts, annual return and a corporation tax return. Limited Companies are only taxed on their profits (usually at a rate of 20%) and as such are not subject to the higher (personal) tax rates placed on sole traders or partnerships which can reach 40%.

The main advantage is that the company has limited liability and so the owner(s) are not personally liable for debts. A private company's liability is limited to the value of the shares owned by its members (called shareholders). In effect, this is normally the money that they have put into the company. Each member's liability is for the original value of the shares they were issued with. However, this is not always as good as it sounds, many banks and other lenders may be reluctant to lend to a limited company precisely because liability is limited. To safeguard against risk lenders may insist on director's guarantees, which may for example mean using personal assets such as houses as security (collateral) for loans.

The above describes a *private* limited company as opposed to a public limited company which is described later in the chapter. A private limited company is usually small and is distinguished by having Ltd. after its name. Shares cannot be sold without the agreement of other shareholders and they are not listed on the stock exchange and shares cannot be advertised or sold to the public.

Franchising, social enterprise, lifestyle businesses, online businesses

Franchising is the granting of a license by one person (the franchisor) to another (the franchisee). This entitles the franchisee to own and operate their own business using the original brand, resources and existing business model of the franchisor. Famous brand names which commonly operate a franchise system include McDonald's, Subway, KFC and the Body Shop. Each franchised branch is owned and operated by the franchisee. However, the franchisor (parent business) retains control over the way in which products and services are marketed and sold, and controls the quality and standards of the business.

To obtain a franchise a payment is made to the original business, the amount will vary according to the size and prestige of the franchise. A McDonald's franchise currently costs between £125,000 and £325,000. There are also many much smaller and less well known franchise companies, with initial investment costs of less than £10,000. For **the franchisor** this is a relatively inexpensive and rapid way of expanding, **the franchisee** provides much of the finance and then takes the responsibility for setting up and running the business. The franchisor may receive a regular management fee and/or a share of the profits as well as a mark-up on any supplies and merchandise. The franchisee has to get supplies from the original company and stick to their products. Someone with a McDonald's franchise cannot use an alternative supplier of cheaper burgers or start to sell sweets and newspapers at the counter. This guarantees quality and consistency, as well as ensuring that sales are created for the franchisor. In return, they will provide training, product development, marketing and advertising, promotional activities and some management services.

The franchisee benefits by operating under the name of the original business, the brand is already known and there should already be brand loyal customers. This should be easier than trying to establish an unknown business. In theory a franchise business is less likely to fail because of the support of the original business, this may mean that lenders are more willing to supply funds.

On the other hand the franchisee has much less control and freedom than with an independent business, for example in the sourcing of supplies. Operating a franchise can also be expensive and the franchisor will expect a cut of the profits.

A **social enterprise** is a revenue-generating business with social or environmental objectives. It will have a clear sense of its 'social mission': which means it will know what difference it is trying to make, who it aims to help, and how it plans to do it. Its income is generated through selling goods or services, and profits are reinvested in its social objectives in the business or in the community, rather than being paid to shareholders and owners. They are not charities, but profit making business enterprises designed to further social aims.

Social enterprises cover a wide range of activities, Cafédirect is the UK's largest Fairtrade hot drinks company; The Big Issue, the Eden Project and Jamie Oliver's restaurant Fifteen are all examples of social enterprises. According to the government there are approximately 70,000 social enterprises in the UK, contributing £18.5 billion to the UK economy and employing almost a million people.

A **lifestyle business** is a small business in which the owner is more anxious to pursue interests that reflect his or her lifestyle rather than to make a sizeable profit. A lifestyle business is a business in which the entrepreneur's aim is to make a reasonable living and have the freedom to do all the things they want at a time of their choosing. Therefore a lifestyle business can be almost anything, an art gallery, a potter's studio, a book-shop, vintage car restoration or a business organising walking holidays, they are all run by people that care about their chosen field and not just run for purely financial reasons.

Growth to PLC and stock market flotation

A successful business that grows may decide to make the transition from a limited company to a Public Limited company (plc). To become a plc, a business needs to go through the process of a stock market flotation. A stock market flotation involves selling a percentage of your business in the form of shares on one of the stock markets. The main market is the London Stock Exchange, which is mostly for large companies. Smaller companies may go to the Alternative Investment Market (AIM), a sub-market of the London Stock Exchange, which has a more flexible regulatory system than the main market.

Floating on the stock exchange can be both costly and time-consuming but for many businesses the advantages outweigh the initial obstacles. When a business decides to go public it will get an independent valuation and then decide what proportion of shares to sell. This may be influenced by how much money the business wants to raise, this may be for expansion, moving overseas or to pay back a venture capital investor.

The main benefits of becoming a plc are the access to new capital to develop and expand the business and to realise initial investments for the owners of the business. It can raise the public profile of the business, providing reassurance to customers, suppliers and investors. Employees and managers can be given share options which can encourage and motivate them to improve business performance. It also increases the company's ability to make acquisitions, using listed shares as currency.

Inevitably, there are drawbacks as well. Besides the initial cost of the flotation there are also ongoing costs such as higher professional fees. Public companies have to comply with a wide range of additional regulatory requirements and meet accepted standards of corporate governance. Taking on shareholders means that their interests have to be considered when running the company; these interests may clash with the original owner's objectives.

The owner will have to give up some control of the business; shareholders can use their votes to influence company direction. They will also expect a dividend and for the company to perform well enough to maintain and increase the value of their investment. There is also a risk that the company can face a takeover bid and an aggressively built up large shareholding. In addition, the financial markets are subject to fluctuations brought about by market sentiment and economic conditions. These can be damaging to a business with a falling share price.

Shawbrook

The specialist lender Shawbrook which provides loans to small and medium-sized businesses has been valued at £725m in a stock market flotation. Shawbrook, priced its initial public offering at 290p per share and said it expected to raise £90m from the flotation. It sold 75m shares, or about 30% of its equity.

Its chief executive, Richard Pyman, said Shawbrook would be able to grow and become a better-known name in specialist business banking. He said: "Our aim is to drive further growth by maximising opportunities in existing markets, and developing a range of products to facilitate expansion into adjacent segments."

Fat Face

The high-street fashion brand Fat Face abandoned its flotation on the UK stock market after a lack of demand for the shares. The flotation was expected to raise £110m. Currently, the company has 208 stores around the UK and Ireland. Advisers to the company are said to have informed board members that there was insufficient demand at the price at which it wanted to sell shares to investors.

What advantages are there for Shawbrook in becoming a plc?

What possible disadvantages might there be?

What likely problems might the failed flotation cause Fat Face in the short term?

What likely problems might the failed flotation cause Fat Face in the long term?

Chapter 23

Business choices

Health spending

It is tempting to make the emotive statement that everyone should have access to unlimited treatment as health is so important. However, using resources for health means that alternatives must be given up, and keeping pace with growing demand would be very difficult. Many developed countries have a growing proportion of elderly people. Old people require more health care. Expectations are rising: more people now want cosmetic surgery to improve their appearance, for example. Medical advances make more new and expensive treatments available: Kadcyla, a new drug for breast cancer treatment, costs £90,000 per patient.

Choices between spending on health and other priorities mean that some options must be given up. Once a total health budget is set, more Kadcyla (for example) means less spending elsewhere. Many decisions, in life and in business, entail choices.

Businesses need to make choices; they do not have sufficient resources to do everything they would like to. A bakery may want to install new ovens and buy a new delivery van but it cannot afford both at once. If it decides that the new ovens are more important, it will have sacrificed or given up the opportunity to buy the van at that time. This idea is the principle that lies behind opportunity cost. It is something that governments, businesses, and individuals use all the time whether they realise it or not.

Besides choosing what to consume, individuals also choose how to organise their lives around work, leisure and other commitments. Opportunity cost is about time as well as resources. Furthermore, it applies to any human organisation.

Opportunity cost

Simply stated, an opportunity cost is the cost of the best missed alternative when a choice is made. It is what has had to be given up in order to do something else. For example you may be faced with the choice on a Friday night of going out with friends or staying in and studying. You cannot do both, if you decide to go out you have given up the opportunity to stay in and study. The opportunity cost of going out is staying in.

For a business, the opportunity cost might refer to the profit a company could have earned from using its resources in a different way. In theory a business will leave an industry when it can make more profit in another line of work, in other words the business will change when the opportunity cost exceeds its present return.

> Using any limited resource in one way means we sacrifice alternative uses. The best alternative given up is called the **opportunity cost**.

When a business start-up is being planned, and also when an established business is planning new product developments, there will be opportunity costs to consider. Going for one particular product means that it will not be possible also to develop an alternative. The opportunity cost of one product will be the potential profit foregone by not going ahead with a different product. It will often be possible to identify a range of possible new business activities, only one of which can be actively pursued.

Many businesses consciously consider opportunity cost when formulating strategy. Exploring the relative profitability of several different ideas will be important in the planning process. Alongside this, the business will consider the enthusiasm and commitment that the owners, the managers and key employees can bring to the development process. This may be strong enough to make the opportunity cost of alternatives seem quite low, even if it is potentially profitable.

An accountant does not take opportunity cost into consideration but an economist does. Consider the example of an office manager who leaves a job where she earned a salary of £35,000 in order to start a small garden design business. In her first year of trading she makes a profit of £20,000. The accountant is pleased that she has made a profit in her first year of trading, however the economist sees an opportunity cost of £15,000, the amount she has given up to pursue her new career.

The concept of opportunity cost can be applied to many different situations, whenever choices have to be made between competing alternatives. Opportunity cost is usually defined in terms of money, but it may also be considered in terms of time, person-hours, mechanical output, or any other finite resource.

> **Think!**
>
> What is the immediate opportunity cost of your reading this today?
>
> What is the opportunity cost of having chosen Business?
>
> Who can you think of who has given up a really attractive alternative by making a choice?

Choices and potential trade-offs

A trade-off is a situation where having more of one thing leads to having less of another. It is linked to the concept of opportunity cost. We often think about opportunity cost in an either/or situation, where we must choose one thing over another. A trade-off involves a situation where two things can be traded against each other, where more of one choice leaves less of the alternative. It is necessary to balance how much of each option is chosen, but not to sacrifice either of them completely.

> **Think!**
>
> Can you visualise examples of where businesses face a trade-off between:
>
> Manufacturing costs and quality
>
> Worker motivation and wage costs
>
> Taking risks and potential reward?

For example, if you face a straightforward choice between staying in on a Friday night or going out, your decision will involve opportunity cost. If you stay in the opportunity cost is not going out. However if you look at this choice throughout the year there is a trade-off between the amount of time you spend studying to get a good grade and the total time spent socialising. More time spent going out means less time with your books and perhaps not as good a grade!

Businesses face trade-offs all the time as well. There is for example, a trade-off between money spent on developing new products and money spent promoting existing ones. The business will have a certain level of finance available for promotion and more of one will mean less of the other.

> **Think!**
>
> Young professionals face a trade-off between commitment to their jobs and their social life. They frequently accept working for very long hours early in their careers, but find the trade-off against other activities harder as years go by. Can you understand this? Is it likely to apply to you?

Within a business, departments will try to calculate the costs and benefits of promotional activity in order to argue their respective cases to senior managers. Market researchers will need to estimate likely future sales revenue, using all the information they can get. Senior managers must then decide how the available funding is shared.

> Like opportunity cost, a **trade-off** involves choice. We often use the term trade-off when looking at a balance between two choices, choosing more of one and less of the other, rather than making a simple either/or choice.

When contemplating a business start-up, there may be a significant trade-off to be considered because the work involved may mean losing time spent with family or on recreational activities. Being self-employed often means having to work longer hours than an employer would require. Someone who values working independently and/or creatively will often have to trade off some income and perhaps security against freedom to do what pleases them most.

When a sole proprietor business becomes a public limited company, the owner gains limited liability and often also receives a cash injection to the business from share sales. These benefits are traded-off against some reduction in control and the need to share future profits with other shareholders.

When undertaking market research, businesses often face a trade-off between time and expense on one hand and the quality of information received on the other. Given the normal shape of a demand curve, businesses are forced to trade-off a bigger profit margin from a higher price against a greater volume of sales from a lower price.

Tiffany Rose is a UK fashion label that makes designer clothes for pregnant women.

Tiffany was working as a marketing manager for a London law firm when she was inspired to start her own business by the difficulties her pregnant sister was having in finding an elegant dress to wear to a wedding. Tiffany started the business at her kitchen table in 2003 and it is now a multi-million pound operation.

As the mother of young children, Tiffany had to find her work-time where she could: "I became very used to getting a day's work done between 7pm and midnight. It wasn't great for the social life, but I was very lucky to have an incredibly supportive husband."

Explain the opportunity costs for Tiffany of setting up her own business.

What sort of trade-offs might she have experienced?

Chapter 24

Moving from entrepreneur to leader

Travis Kalanick

In 1998 Kalanick dropped out of his degree course to co-found Scour Inc. and Scour Exchange, a search engine and a peer-to-peer file sharing service. Faced with lawsuits for copyright infringement from the film and music industries, Scour filed for bankruptcy in 2000.

In 2001, he co-founded Red Swoosh, another peer-to-peer file sharing service. This was sold to Akamai Technologies for $19m in 2007.

In 2009 Kalanick and Garrett Camp founded Uber, which is a mobile application that connects passengers with vehicles for hire. In essence Uber uses web technology to build an alternative to traditional taxi services. Uber has faced criticism, for example over customer safety issues and its circumvention of some of the regulations traditional competitors face. However, it now operates in over 100 cities, thriving in many of them. Kalanick's net worth is estimated at $5.3bn.

Kalanick has been described as a serial entrepreneur, someone who sets up businesses, sells them and starts again. He might now stay with Uber, but he might not once growth slows. He is seen as a supporter of the 'Cult of Disruption' which sets out to challenge bloated industries and regulation. His approach is summed up by one quote: "Whatever it is you're afraid of, go after it."

Discussion points

What makes Travis Kalanick a successful start-up entrepreneur?

Are these same qualities required for long-term business leadership?

Is challenging regulation always appropriate?

The difficulties in developing from an entrepreneur

Travis Kalanick has many of the entrepreneurial characteristics which were identified in Chapter 20. These were hard working, motivation, risk taking, initiative, creativity, resilience, perseverance and understanding their market. In new businesses and small businesses, one person can drive the activity onwards with a combination of these characteristics.

Many entrepreneurs make the mistake of thinking that because they have shown the necessary qualities to come up with a valid idea and then start a business, they will also be able to lead the company forward. Leadership though, is a different thing altogether.

All of the entrepreneurial characteristics can be evident in individual behaviour; they tell us little about interpersonal skills. As an extreme case, there are some intelligent and entrepreneurial people who also have limited social skills, struggling to relate to other people. Good leaders need emotional intelligence and interpersonal skills, entrepreneurs might succeed without these things.

Emotional intelligence

The core of **emotional intelligence** combines recognising the impact of our own emotions on our feelings and actions with considering other people's emotions and feelings when interacting with them.

As a simplification, the ability to empathise is at the heart of emotional intelligence. Understanding people and how to get the best out of them is an important skill for leadership. At best, this extends to understanding the leader's own feelings, attitudes and biases as well. So, for example, an entrepreneur might have a strong vision but might lack the skills to enthuse others. An emotionally intelligent leader should be more capable of building a shared vision which the people s/he works with commit to and pursue together.

2014 UK Business Woman of the year, Harriet Green, was CEO at Thomas Cook. The travel business had been struggling and losing market share. The Business Woman award citation referred to "reform through strategy, technology and high performing teams." By the time of the award, the Thomas Cook share price had risen by 950% since her arrival. Harriet Green is clearly an effective leader. In mid-2015, damage to the Thomas Cook brand from badly handled publicity about a holiday tragedy came after Harriet Green had left the business.

At the same ceremony, Jenny Dawson of 'Rubies from the Rubble' won the 'New Generation' award. Jenny started with determination to address the issue of the tonnes of fresh fruit and vegetables which were discarded whilst still in good condition. The practical solution which Rubies from the Rubble have developed is to transform perishable foods into durable chutneys. After rapid initial expansion, Jenny is now leading reorganisation. For example, some production is now being outsourced to capture economies of scale. The skills required of Jenny have moved well beyond the initial entrepreneurial flair.

Delegation

As a business grows, it becomes impossible for one individual to keep control of all decision taking. Delegating tasks to others becomes necessary. To be successful this requires subordinates with appropriate skills and attitudes who have been suitably prepared to accept authority. Delegation results in an organisational structure as described in Chapter 16. Having delegated functions and authority, a good leader balances a supportive role against being too interfering. This is not always easy for an entrepreneur used to being in charge of everything.

Table 24.1: Advantages of delegation

Benefit	Concise meaning
Load sharing	The stress on top managers is reduced as more decisions are shared
Job satisfaction	Having authority can boost motivation
Specialisation	A narrower focus allows people to make more informed decisions
Flexibility	Easier to respond rapidly to changing conditions
Progression	Experience of delegated authority equips people for promotion

Delegation is the passing down of authority from a superior to a subordinate.

Trust and verification

"He who does not trust enough will not be trusted." – Lao Tzu

"Trust, but verify." – Ronald Reagan

A lack of trust is unhealthy for relationships, whether in business or elsewhere in life. Someone to whom authority has been delegated will hope to be allowed to do things without a supervisor breathing down their neck. At the same time, higher level managers who have delegated will retain senior responsibility and will not become disinterested. At one level, there appears to be a trade-off here. To what extent should delegated responsibility be supervised?

> Nick Leeson became general manager of a future markets operation on the Singapore Exchange for Barings Bank. Initial successes brought £10m profit for Barings and a £130,000 bonus for Leeson in his first year. When his luck changed, he used an 'error account' to hide losses. These losses reached £208m by the end of 1994. A trade basically gambling that the Tokyo Exchange would be stable overnight was undone by the Kobe earthquake in January 1995. Taking bigger risks trying to recoup losses led eventually to Barings' losses totalling £827m.
>
> The Bank became insolvent. Leeson had not been adequately supervised.

Verification essentially involves reviewing, inspecting and testing to check performance levels. Constant verification can be read as implying a lack of trust. More positively, validation can be seen as giving recognition for success – something people welcome. Everyone likes to be reassured that they have done well. Validation is often part of appraisal, a process of checking people's progress in their roles, identifying appropriate training and support, and planning career development.

If the culture is supportive and verification processes blend into validation, it is possible to maintain an atmosphere of trust whilst also keeping informed about progress and any difficulties. One of the challenges for leaders is to develop the relevant skills for this.

> **Verification** is the process of reviewing, inspecting and testing to check the quality of what has been done.
>
> **Validation**, though similar, often contains an element of recognition for work and the worker involved.

Listening and keeping an open mind

> Aspects of an open mind (drawn from Process Excellence Network)
> 1. A personal focus on creativity
> 2. Respecting people and their ability to observe – and find ways to do tasks better
> 3. Working with people who have performance issues or other problems to improve
> 4. Promoting small teams to looking at how they can improve
> 5. Encouraging the people at all levels to come up with ideas
> 6. Working with IT to understand what can be done and talking with staff about what they could do with it to solve problems and increase performance
> 7. Understanding that, in among all the ideas or parts of ideas that fail, there can be gold nuggets of great new ways to improve
> 8. Someone who doesn't know the business can see things in a fresh way

Young people with good ideas can feel thwarted if their ideas are overlooked. Coping with other peoples' ideas being chosen is far harder for an entrepreneur who has led a business to successful growth. Businesses which grow successfully are likely to reach the point where others join the entrepreneur in running the business.

If the entrepreneur has a belief that s/he knows best, this is likely to lead to a closed mind. Even fully hearing out someone with contrasting ideas is difficult with this mind set. This can mean that crucial information and good ideas are overlooked. It can also demotivate people in the business and so lead to a reduction in the quality of their performance. The business is likely to become less capable of responding to changing circumstances and new opportunities.

Good leaders accumulate available information and ideas, at the same time empowering people around them by listening carefully and seeking to understand fully. The 'synthesising' process of pulling together ideas from a range of sources can often contribute valuably to decision making. It also contributes to a healthy pattern of open two way communication in the business.

While leadership qualities may be something certain individuals are apparently born with, the reality is that leadership skills are developed over time and through experience. To become a leader entrepreneurs have to develop the key skills of leadership. They have to be able to distance themselves from the business and focus on long term aims rather than the day to day problems. Part of being a leader is the ability to give others direction and to inspire and motivate them to reach their full potential. Finally, a good leader sometimes needs to be able to make tough decisions for the good of the business without being swayed by emotion or personal friendships.

Henry Ford

Henry Ford, who founded the Ford Motor Company in 1903, was in many ways ahead of his time. He hired African-Americans, women and disabled people long before most other business owners did and believed in the principle of paying good wages to attract and keep the best workers. An inspiring and hugely successful leader himself, he had much to say on the subject...

"If there is any one secret of success, it lies in the ability to get the other person's point of view and see things from that person's angle as well as from your own."

"You can't build a reputation on what you are going to do."

"A business that makes nothing but money is a poor business."

"Coming together is a beginning; keeping together is progress; working together is success."

Exam style question

Evaluate the importance of emotional intelligence in business leadership.   *(20 marks)*